My Ultimate
MEALTHY
MULTIPOT
Cookbook

100 Surprisingly Delicious Recipes with Illustrations for your Mealthy 9-in-1 pressure cooker

By

Elizabeth Daniels

PAN PACIFIC PRESS

Pan Pacific Press
Santa Monica, CA

Customer Reviews

"This book provides nutrition info with each recipe. That's a huge plus for me (and a potential reduction in my plus-size ;) With such a wide variety of recipes, knowing the amounts of calories, fat, carbs, etc. makes it really helpful and easy to know exactly what I'm eating. Provides a surprisingly wide variety of tasty meals. Loving this book!" - Melanie R.

"I was surprised you could cook an entire roasted chicken in this machine. It's way more than a just a rice cooker and steamer. Thanks for making this. These kinds of foodie discoveries are really fun." – Tom S.

"This book covers a wide reach with some seriously great recipes. My husband L O V E D The Bar-B-Q ribs (they were tasty) I fell for the Dijon Chicken with mushrooms and we are just getting started. I've never tired rice pudding before so I'm looking forward to that and a lot of other meals I've never known how to cook" - Rachel C

"Great for beginners! I like the clear instructions, serving sizes and nutritional info...the range of recipes is impressive and helps me keep my family of 5 looking forward to dinner time." - Liz E.

Legal Notice

All content herein represents the author's own experiences and opinions. The information written, illustrated and presented in this book is for the purpose of entertainment only.

Although we are big fans, neither the author nor Pan Pacific Press are associated with Mealthy or Multipot.

The author does not assume any liability for the use of or inability to use any or all of the information contained in this book, and does not accept responsibility for any type of loss or damage that may be experienced by the user as the result of activities occurring from the use of any information in this book. Use the information at your own risk.

The author reserves the right to make changes he or she deems required to future versions of the publication to maintain accuracy.

PAN PACIFIC PRESS

Published in the United States of America by Pan Pacific Press

www.Pan-PacificPress.com

Want a FREE Cookbook?

Then join the
Book Review Club!

(It's Free for readers like you)

Get your first free cookbook today
at this link:

www.JoinTheBookReviewClub.com/a2

Table Of Contents

WHY YOU NEED THIS BOOK!   13

ALL ABOUT PROGRAMMABLE PRESSURE COOKING   21

HOW TO USE YOUR MULTIPOT COOKER   27

PRO TIPS   37

MAIN COURSE   43

   Ginger Sesame Roasted Pork   *44*

   Country Style BBQ Ribs   *46*

   Dijon Chicken with Farro and Mushrooms   *48*

   Shrimp with Lemon Risotto   *50*

   Jambalaya   *52*

   Pad Thai   *54*

   Massaman Chicken   *56*

   Balsamic Roast Beef with Rustic Vegetables   *57*

   Whole Roasted Chicken   *58*

   Pineapple Chicken Fajitas   *60*

   One Pot Teriyaki Chicken and Vegetables   *62*

   Vegetarian Portobello Pot Roast   *64*

   Hawaiian Fried Rice   *66*

   General Tso's Chicken   *68*

   Super-Easy Spanish Paella   *70*

Rice Cooker Mahi Mahi   72

Honey Bourbon Chicken   73

RICE RECIPES (White/Brown/Basmati/Multi-Grain...etc.)   75

The Perfect Sushi Rice   76

Rice Cooker Pasta   77

Spanish Rice   78

Brown Rice   79

Multigrain Rice   80

Cauliflower Rice   82

Vegetable Rice   83

No Fuss Beans   84

Basmati Rice   85

Quick and Easy Lentils   86

VEGETABLE AND SIDE DISH RECIPES   89

Steamed Broccoli   90

Quinoa and Pomegranate Salad   91

Cuban Black Beans and Rice   92

Cheesy Polenta   93

Cheesy Jalapeno Bread   94

Rice Cooker Bread   96

Steamed Artichokes   97

Mediterranean Quinoa Salad with Red Wine Vinaigrette   98

Garlic Mashed Potatoes   100

Potato Salad   102

Sweet Potatoes   104

Hummus   105

BREAKFAST RECIPES 107

Vanilla Yogurt Parfait 108

Giant Rice Cooker Pancake with Maple Syrup and Berry Compote 110

Sausage and Grits Breakfast Casserole 112

Hard Boiled Eggs 114

Whole Grain Porridge 115

Huevos Rancheros 116

Old Fashioned Oatmeal 117

Slow-Cooked Blueberry French Toast 118

Western Omelette Quiche 120

Rice Cooker Summer Vegetable Frittata 121

LUNCH RECIPES 123

Buddha Bowl 124

Chipotle Chicken Bowls with Cilantro Lime Rice 126

Lemon Chicken with Zucchini Noodles 128

BBQ Pork Chops with Steamed Apples 129

Orange Chicken 130

Garlic Drumsticks 132

Steamed Dumplings with Asian Salad 133

Mongolian Beef 134

Beef Gyros 136

Tavern Burgers 138

Jacket Potatoes 139

Egg Mayo Sandwiches 140

Pulled Chicken Tacos 141

Beefy Broccoli Noodles and Cheese 142

Rice Cooker Braised Chicken Wings   *143*

Mango Cucumber Rice Salad   *144*

SOUPS, CHILI, STEWS, SOUFFLES   147

Rice Cooker Chili   *148*

Taco Soup   *149*

White Chicken Chili   *150*

Chicken Daikon Soup   *151*

Hearty Red Wine Stew   *152*

Butternut Cauliflower Soup   *153*

Pho   *154*

Beef and Guinness Stew   *156*

Beef Barley Soup   *158*

Creamy Tomato Soup   *159*

Potato Leek Soup   *160*

DESSERTS   163

Self-Saucing Banana Pudding   *164*

Chocolate Lava Cake   *165*

Banana Bread   *166*

Poached Pomegranate Spiced Pears   *167*

Rice Cooker Tatin Cake (Apple Upside Down Cake)   *168*

Green Tea Matcha Cake   *169*

Rice Pudding   *170*

Lemon Lime Polenta Cake with Yogurt Icing   *171*

Chocolate Fondue   *172*

Japanese Mochi   *173*

Easy Flan   *174*

KID-FRIENDLY RECIPES   177

Chili Mac   178

Mac N' Cheese   179

Spaghetti and Meatballs   180

Applesauce   181

Baked Beans   182

Corn On The Cob   183

Bacon Ranch Potatoes   184

Sloppy Joes   185

Homemade Chicken Soup   186

Pizza Pasta   187

Lasagna   188

Pizza Pull-Apart Bread   189

Chili Dogs   190

1

WHY YOU NEED THIS BOOK!

Save Time with Our Illustrated Quick Start Guide

Kitchen appliances have come a long way since the scary, rattling pressure cookers your grandma used to use. You can now program them with the touch of a button and walk away. With our Quick Start Guide, you won't have to read through endless confusing instructions we all skip anyway. You can enjoy time without watching the stove because today they do all the work for us. You'll be able to easily understand the digital controls, parts, and instructions, and be on your way to healthy, fun family meals in no time. The best part about this book is how we'll show you the Mealthy MultiPot Pressure Cooker doesn't only cook rice—you can whip up delicious one-pot meals and gourmet delights right in the comfort of your own kitchen in a fraction of the time it takes to cook in a traditional oven. And of course, we make sure you'll get your MultiPot to create the most perfectly fluffy and delicious rice in just half the time.

Unbiased Real-World Instructions and Recipes You Won't Find in Any MultiPot Rice Cooker and Food Steamer Manual

With this book, you'll get decadent and delicious meals having your taste buds thinking you're eating dishes prepared by a gourmet chef. You'll find handy customized recipes that help you easily convert cups in lieu of only using the smaller measuring cup that comes with the MULTIPOT. All the meals are easy to prepare with detailed, easy-to-follow instructions that won't have you curious, which settings to use let alone how long to cook meat and rice at the same time. You won't find tips and tricks like how to crisp meals inside a rice steamer in just any cookbook. With the MultiPot cooker, also gone are the long cooking times of your grandma's pressure cooker and the days of boring one pot meals. This cookbook has you covered.

100 Amazing Recipes Not Found in Other Cookbooks

This book also offers you 100 amazing recipes not found in any other Mealthy MultiPot Pressure Cooker cookbook. These unique and easy to prepare recipes elevate your breakfast, lunch, dinner, and desserts to a whole new level. If you love one pot, easy meals that can put dinner on the table with the push of a button this cookbook is for you. You'll learn how to cook rice and meat at the same time, so you're cooking time is cut in half. Prepare healthy dishes and meals for your family with the power of steam. We'll also include Kid-Friendly recipes that will have the little ones wanting to get in on all the kitchen fun. From comforting meats, soups and stews to refreshing salads and decadent desserts—this book offers you 100 amazing recipes that will have everyone in the family wanting to use the Mealthy MultiPot Pressure Cooker.

Pro Tips to Get the Most from Your Mealthy MultiPot Pressure Cooker

Not only will you get detailed, easy-to-use instructions and 100 mouthwatering recipes—you'll get our pro tips and tricks to help you get the most out of your Mealthy MultiPot. You'll be surprised at what and just how much this amazing appliance can do! This book will teach you how to cook meals for later, saving you even more time. These pro tips help you find all the things not normally associated with pressure cookers, so you make the perfect meal every time. Whether pressurized or not, we put together the most comprehensive set of tips included with 100 recipes of some succulently, surprising things you can make in the Mealthy MultiPot Pressure Cooker.

How to Avoid Common Mistakes and Start Cooking Like a Pro

This book is so comprehensive and thorough, that you'll learn how to avoid common mistakes and start cooking like a pro in no time. No more burning or scorching food you walked away from! With the Mealthy MultiPot Pressure Cooker, you'll not only learn how to cook perfect rice, this book will teach you how to avoid mistakes when cooking other grains like brown and multigrain rice, as well as quinoa. You learn how to perfectly steam meat, as well as kid-friendly pasta and fun recipes. You'll never scorch your favorite fish, pork, chicken, or beef again. You'll even learn how to keep those gooey, cheesy one-pot meals from sticking to the lid in your Mealthy MultiPot Pressure Cooker.

The Most Comprehensive Book Written for the MultiPot Rice Cooker and Food Steamer

Looking to cook up the most healthy, nutritious meals on the planet? You'll be able to do just that and most importantly save time with your Mealthy MultiPot. In this book, with this product, you'll find more simple-to-use instructions, guides, pro tips, recipes and MultiPot knowledge than all of those other more complex books and cooker manuals. We break things down and make them so super simple that even your senior family members will be able to use this kitchen appliance with ease. Not only will you get all of the information needed in a simple, easy to use guide—you'll get 100 mouthwatering recipes to help you master your Mealthy MultiPot Pressure Cooker.

Gourmet Tips to Cook Perfectly Cooked, Delicious Rice

Of course, you won't just get 100 amazing recipes—we've included scrumptious gourmet tips to have you cooking perfectly delicious rice every time you use your Mealthy MultiPot! Not only rice, but think soups, salads, stews, and delicious one pot meals. You'll learn how to perfect sushi rice, make your own multigrain rice dishes, and just how to use them in your favorite salads, soups, and meals. You'll learn how to elevate meals for breakfast like yogurt parfaits and french toast. That's right you can even cook breakfast dishes like yogurt, french toast, and pancakes in your Mealthy MultiPot.

Several Paleo, Diabetic-Friendly, and Gluten-Free Recipes Included

One of the most amazing details about the Mealthy MultiPot Pressure Cooker is all the healthy meals you'll be able to serve up! Our recipes will have gourmet tips that help you whip up paleo, diabetic-friendly, and gluten-free recipes too! We'll you learn easy conversion tips that help you transform your favorite dietary lifestyle into a foodie's dream. With this recipe book, on the Mealthy MultiPot Pressure Cooker, you'll be able to understand just how to convert ingredients in order to make delicious vegan and vegetarian dishes in your cooker. That's how comprehensive this book is when it comes to mastering food prepared in the Mealthy MultiPot Pressure Cooker.

2

ALL ABOUT PROGRAMMABLE PRESSURE COOKING

A Brief History of the Programmable Pressure Cooker

Historians haven't quite figured out exactly who invented this genius kitchen appliance, but on January 9th, 1991, the Chinese scientist, Mr. Yong-Guang Wang, filed the first electric pressure cooker patent. While this is the best ways to cook instant, fluffy, restaurant-quality rice directly in your own home, the Mealthy MultiPot Pressure Cooker is a multi-dish device that doesn't just focus on 'rice & steaming'. This electric pressure cooker instructs the chef on several ways to cook food at once such as simmering, braising, slow cooking, warming, and stewing by using different combinations of cooking temperature, pressure and cooking times which has since led to the new era of electric pressure cookers such as the Mealthy MultiPot Pressure Cooker.

The Immense Variety of Dishes Programmable Pressure Cookers Create!

You can whip up quick and easy breakfasts in the morning, so you can curb that morning stop on your commute and start the day with more healthy meals like yogurt parfait, old-fashioned oatmeal, veggie frittatas, quiche, and even hard-boiled eggs. Lunch is made much more simple with this electric pressure cooker too! You can easily create fast healthy dishes like Buddha Bowls, Pad Thai, Jacket Potatoes, and Chicken Tacos. Dinners, desserts and snacks, and beyond are all made more simple with the Mealthy MultiPot Pressure Cooker. Think Pho, Chocolate Lava Cake, Mac N' Cheese, Chili Dogs and Whole Roasted Chicken. All fast, healthy, and absolutely delicious!

Health Benefits of Cooking with the Mealthy MultiPot Pressure Cooker

The Mealthy MultiPot Pressure Cooker offers you a vast array of health benefits. Not only will you be cooking clean and only adding the oil necessary to keep the dish from sticking, you'll learn how to really make each dish in its healthiest cooking style possible. Electric pressure cookers cut preservatives, GMOs, and other unhealthy additives. You'll be cooking food as naturally as possible, just like many pro chefs. Pressure cooking is also diet friendly. Not just any diet, but great for people who are trying to lower their cholesterol and blood pressure.

Amazing for anyone wanting to cut fat and sugar. Vegetarians, Vegans, Paleo can all create delicious meals with the Mealthy MultiPot Pressure Cooker. Along with rice, you can steam veggies for paleo, vegan or carb-watching diets—as well as meats, pasta, and other delicious grains like quinoa.

Why Pro Chefs Use Programmable Pressure Cookers

You can cook like a pro chef right in your own home because with foods pressurized all the various flavors are infused directly back into the food and succulently seal in the flavor. This transcends the flavor of each meal you cook at home while the cooking time goes from the traditional 30 to 10 minutes on each meal. Minimal cleaning is required and it's super fun to use at home. The electric pressure cooker is adored by pro chefs, as well as busy parents and students for its programmable features and ease of use. Professional chefs love the speed of cooking with a pressure cooker and now technology has afforded it so you can cook like a pro chef right in the comfort of home!

The Difference Between an Electric Rice Cooker and Pressure Cooker

The electric rice cooker and pressure cooker usually look almost exactly the same. Many people often wonder exactly what the difference is when it comes to cooking with both appliances. While they both cook food at an incredibly quick rate of time, they are actually very different. Both appliances cook using steam, but that's the only thing these two have in common. The electric rice cooker uses a heating coil or pad with an inner pot and lid. Sometimes they come with steaming baskets, sometimes they don't. Rice is cooked using liquid, like water, that evaporates and turns into steam that the rice absorbs causing the rice to become fluffy and soft. The pressure cooker is similar to the rice cooker but is designed with a sensor on the lid that is sealable so steam cannot escape and cooks the food with a combination of heat and pressure. Most electric rice cookers are programmable and often much easier to use while being able to cook a vast array of tantalizing meals and flavorful dishes.

3

HOW TO USE YOUR MULTIPOT COOKER

How to Get Started in 2 Minutes!

Add rice. Add at least 1 cup of water. Push a button. That's how simple it is to get started using your Mealthy Multipot 9-in-1 Programmable Cooker. Use the power button to get started. Make sure you read all of the instructions carefully before the first use. Make sure your Multipot is on a flat surface with nothing underneath the stainless steel surface! Be sure to use your Multipot 9-in-1 Programmable Cooker only on a level, dry and heat-resistant surface. Line up the arrows on the pot and lid and turn the lid until it clicks. Turn the valve to sealing. Click preset buttons to cycle through high, medium and low settings. The red floater will raise when the pot comes to pressure. When the cook time is complete the Multipot will shift to KEEP WARM mode. Here, you can carefully release the pressure manually using an oven glove or let the pressure naturally release. You'll know pressure is released when the red floater falls down, flush with the pot.

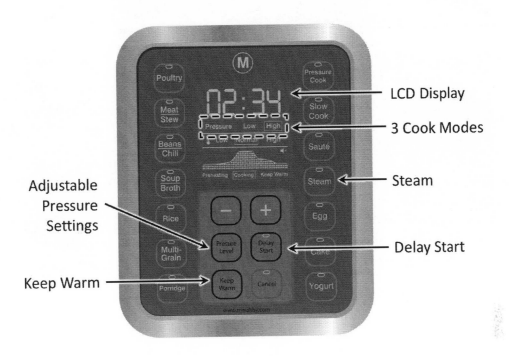

Overview of Buttons, Timer, and Settings

The buttons and timers are super easy to learn. With every recipe, you'll learn just how to cook each meal to perfection. There's a button for flash cooking white rice automatically. One for cooking fluffy, delicious brown rice and grains that require longer cooking times. The steam button is great for steaming vegetables and other delicious main dishes. While the delay timer can help you cook the most tantalizing meals when you're super-busy or aren't even at home. You can also use the keep warm button so your food remains fresh and hot until your dinner guests or family has arrived, or if dinner gets postponed. You really can get started in two minutes with the Mealthy MultiPot Pressure Cooker—for delicious, healthy, pro chef style meals right at home. The best part about the Mealthy MultiPot are all the accessories that come with this pressure cooker. No other model on the market offers you pot holders perfectly sized to pick up the inner pot and a trivet to elevate vegetables out of the water for easier steaming.

Overview of How to Cook Rice, Soups, Stews, Vegetables, and More

Rice is easy to cook using the 8 step process below. Many soup and stew recipes will require you to use the timer function in order to avoid burning the soup. You'll want to set the time that each dish needs to steam. Your Mealthy MultiPot Pressure Cooker will begin to countdown once water reaches a boil. Then it will shut off once the time has elapsed. The best part about this rice cooker is that it automatically switches over to keep your food warm once your dish is finished cooking. That way you can count on perfect, fluffy rice every single time you cook. Soups will never scorch again. Dishes won't stick to lids or burn. Vegetables won't wilt, but be cooked to steamed perfection.

How to Clean and Store your Mealthy MultiPot Pressure Cooker

Allow the appliance to cool before starting the cleaning process. Unplug your Mealthy MultiPot from the electric outlet before cleaning. On occasion, there may be residue in the bottom of the cooker. While this is almost always unavoidable, you can easily clean the appliance in no time at all. Simply pour a few inches of water into the bottom of the Cooker/Steamer. If available put a few drops of lemon inside and then cycle it through cooking again on steam. The boiling water will loosen up any remaining residue and help you easily wipe it clean with a damp cloth. Do not use harsh abrasive cleaners, scouring pads or products that are not considered safe to use on nonstick coatings, as this will discolor or ruin the inner pot and accessories. Simply store your rice cooker in a dry place.

Optimal Sizes of Food, How to Time and Avoid Overcooking, Other Necessary Tools

Food sizes can vary, and it is especially useful to follow the recipes to the exact measurement. This will help you avoid overfilling and overcooking your meals. The timer and cooking specifications on each recipe will also help you avoid overcooking food. Tools that come with the Mealthy MultiPot Pressure Cooker like the steam tray, spatula, and measuring cup can come in very handy. The included measuring cup equals one quarter cup of water will yield up to 8 cups of rice.

The ribbed spatula is great when lifting rice out your rice cooker to keep it from falling all over the place. A great pro tip: add a 1/2 tsp. olive oil to rice to avoid bubbling over. Remember that food expands as you cook in your Mealthy MultiPot so never fill it more than 1/2 full or past the maximum fill line.

Do not fill over this line, because food expands while cooking.

Marinating and Prepping Dishes/How to Store Leftovers

Marinating and prepping dishes beforehand are a great way to cook healthy meals in no time. The Mealthy MultiPot is great for making 3-4 meals. Remember to reduce the size of traditional soup or stew recipes for 94-ounce pots and pressure cookers. 64 ounce resealable containers are great for the Mealthy MultiPot. This size container holds 3-4 servings and is perfect for freezing ingredients to quick cook from frozen. If you don't have time to put all of the ingredients together, you can pick a day to meal prep. Freeze in 64-ounce containers and cook a delicious, healthy family meal in no time. When storing leftovers, just place them in resealable containers and refrigerate for up to 72 hours or freeze for up to 14 days.

Never keep rice warm for more than 12 hours. Bacteria can form!

Things to Avoid

Recipes included in this book are easy to follow. Other recipes that use flour when cooking soups may not be ideal for the Mealthy MultiPot Pressure Cooker because they can expand too much and cause overflow or the lid to burst. To protect against electrical shock, do not immerse the appliance in water or any other liquid. When cooking with kids, close supervision is necessary. The cord on the Mealthy MultiPot Pressure Cooker is short in length as to keep it away from hot burners or near a heated oven. When cooking your rice or one-pot meals, do not touch, cover or obstruct the steam vent on the top of the rice cooker as it is extremely hot and may burn your skin. Always make sure the outside of the inner pot is dry before use; if the inner pot is returned to the rice cooker wet, it may damage or cause the product to malfunction. Rice should never be left in the inner pot with the KEEP WARM button on for more than 12 hours.

Detailed 8 Step Process of Using the MultiPot Rice Cooker

1

Using the provided measuring cup, add the desired amount of rice to the inner pot and then place the inner pot into the rice cooker.

2

Rinse your rice to remove excess starch. Fill with water to the line which matches the number of cups of rice being cooked.

3

Press the power button to turn on the Multipot. Press Pressure Cook button and cook for 15 minutes on High pressure.

4

If cooking OTHER RECIPES than rice, select the PRESET button that your recipe calls for.

5

Close the lid securely. The Multipot will begin cooking, and the COOKING INDICATOR LIGHT will illuminate on the display button.

6

The digital display will then show a countdown for the final minutes of cook time.

7

When finished the rice cooker will switch to the KEEP WARM function.

8

When ready to eat, stir the rice to evenly distribute any remaining moisture using the non-slip spatula.

4

PRO TIPS

Not-In-The-Manual Secrets

When it comes to getting that gorgeous color on your meats and vegetables, you'll want to sear it in a pan after you cook it in the Mealthy MultiPot. While the rice cooker takes the long time out of traditional cooking it doesn't have the ability to give your dish or meat that gorgeous, light golden seared color. If you're cooking something like a cheeseburger simply cook it in the rice cooker and heat a frying pan on high. Sear on both sides for 1 to 2 minutes, and you've got one quick delicious meal. When it comes to making yogurt, you'll want to place a ceramic bowl into the bottom of the rice cooker. You'll want to heat your milk and use a candy thermometer to measure the temperature. Simply follow the recipe below and you'll come out with perfect, thick yogurt every time.

Add 1/2 tsp of olive oil to prevent rice from boiling over.

How to Add Crispiness

When it comes to adding crispness to your meal, you'll want to follow the same rule as searing. Because the rice cooker primarily uses steam and hot water to cook food, you won't be able to crisp chicken.

Simply heat a frying pan on high and char for 1 to 2 minutes on each side. Alternatively, you can get that golden brown color in the oven with a broiler. Be sure to heat on high and watch the food so as to not burn it! Occasionally, you may need to brush meats with olive oil to crisp. To keep it healthy, measure out 1 tsp. Olive oil and evenly distribute across one serving. You'll only need 1/2 to 1 tsp. per person/per serving.

Secrets to Making Perfect Fluffy Rice Every Time

The secret to making the perfect, fluffy rice every time you cook in your MultiPot Rice Cooker and Steamer is to use the measuring cup and follow the recipes below. It's that simple. There's no inside tip or trick—just be sure to follow the detailed, yet easy instructions and you'll cook perfect rice in no time—every time! You can also use the rice cooker to flash cook rice in as little as 18 minutes for those really busy days and nights. Just be sure to use the measuring cup that comes with the Mealthy MultiPot Pressure Cooker, and follow the Flash Rice section of the manual included with the appliance. In the event that your rice isn't cooked or hard when the rice cooker switches to KEEP WARM, add 1/2 to 1 cup of water and stir through. Close the lid and press the COOK SWITCH. When the rice cooker switches to KEEP WARM, remove the lid, stir the rice and taste. Repeat as needed until the rice is fluffy and to your desired consistency. If your rice is soggy or full of excess water, stir, replace the lid and leave on KEEP WARM for 10 to 30 minutes longer. Stir occasionally to check until cooked through to desired consistency. If your rice keeps turning brown or caramelizing, simply rinse the rice before cooking to avoid this common kitchen mishap.

Best Way to Safely Reheat Rice

You may have read claims that reheated rice can be loaded with bacteria and possibly cause food poisoning. There is a safe way to reheat rice, and we've got the top pro tips for you here! While you might think a microwave is best, the best way is to add a splash of water to the rice and reheat it using your Mealthy MultiPot Pressure Cooker. Set the timer to 3 to 5 minutes and your rice cooker will fluff and rehydrate your rice in no time. Just make sure it's heated through. In the event that it's not cooked too hot, just add 2 minutes and check it again. Cook until hot and serve with your favorite vegetables, tofu, chicken, pork, shrimp, or beef.

Seasoning Tips for Yellow and Mexican Rice and Other Specialties

Seasoning rice is a healthy way to make more versatile dishes. Adding broth or stock is a great way to elevate the flavor of your rice like a pro chef. The ratio of broth or stock to the Mealthy MultiPot is the same as water to rice ratios on your manual chart or recipe. You can make delicious yellow rice for paella or spanish themed meals by adding a 1/2 tsp. turmeric to the rice cooker and substituting chicken or vegetable broth for water. When creating mexican rice, do the same by substituting chicken broth for water. Add 1 tsp. garlic salt, 1/2 tsp. cumin, 1/2 cup tomato sauce, and 1/4 cup chopped onion. Creating delicious rice dishes in your Mealthy MultiPot has never been so easy! You can find more delicious rice recipes to try below.

Use **Delay Timer** to delay cooking up to 15 hours!

More Juicy Pro-Tips

This book will teach you how to use multiple buttons in the recipes below to cook delicious one pot meals. You can also use the delay timer to cook amazing meals. Simply, press the DELAY TIMER button. Each press is one hour and can be pressed multiple times for increments of 1 to 15 hours. Once the time you need is selected, press the button needed for your recipe. Another helpful pro tip: If you misplace the measuring cup that comes with your Mealthy MultiPot Pressure Cooker, a 3/4 standard US cup is an exact replacement. When turning the rice cooker off: be sure to press the off button twice and unplug the power cord from the electric outlet. Keep in mind that the function of the steam vent is to help pressure cook and steam your food, so hot steam will escape periodically. Simply keep hands, arms and face away from the steam vent to avoid burning yourself. That means little hands too if you tend to have children in the kitchen.

5

MAIN COURSE

Ginger Sesame Roasted Pork

Ginger Sesame Roasted Pork is one of the most tantalizing dishes you can create using the MultiPot Pressure Cooker. Simple easy dinner options that will transform family meals into something out of this world. Serve it up Asian style with rice and steamed vegetables or alongside mashed potatoes and asparagus for a comfort meal twist.

Servings 4-6

Cooking time 30 minutes

Ingredients

1 lb. Pork loin

sea salt

coarse black pepper

1 tsp. sesame oil

3 garlic cloves, chopped

2 tbsp. scallions, thinly sliced

2 tbsp. fresh ginger root, sliced

1 cup soy sauce

2 tsp. sugar or sugar substitute

Instructions

1. Rinse the pork loin and rub generously with sea salt and black pepper.

2. Heat the sesame oil in a non-stick frying pan over medium-high heat. Add the garlic and toast for one minute. Transfer to Aroma rice cooker.

3. Add the pork loin to the frying pan and lightly caramelized on both sides; about 3 to 5 minutes each.

4. Transfer the pork to the rice cooker fat side down. Add scallions, ginger, soy sauce, and sugar. Do not fill the rice cooker with liquid over the top liquid lines to avoid overflowing the rice cooker while cooking.

5. Press the POULTRY button.

6. Leave the lid on and let pork rest in the rice cooker for five minutes. Remove lid, lift pork out with tongs and cut. If pork is still pink in the center, cook for an additional 10 minutes. Serve with your favorite sides.

Nutritional Info: Calories: 221, Sodium: 224 mg, Dietary Fiber: 0.4 g, Fat: 11.3 g, Carbs: 5.4 g, Protein: 23.5 g.

Country Style BBQ Ribs

Mouthwatering Country Style BBQ Ribs have never been so quick and easy! If you love finger-licking ribs, you'll love this yummy meal. While traditional ribs can take hours to make these are done in one hour. Serve with a side of corn on the cob, potato salad, and sweet tea for one authentic, quick southern meal.

Servings 2

Cooking Time 1 hour 10 minutes

Ingredients

1 package Country style ribs, about 5 to 6 ribs

2 tbsp. olive oil

1/3 cup honey

1 tbsp. brown sugar or brown sugar substitute

1 tsp. season salt like Meat Magic Seasoning Salt®

1 (12 oz.) bottle dark beer or stout, like Guinness

1 (16-oz. bottle) barbecue sauce

2 ears of corn, cut in half, husked and rinsed

Instructions

1. Add olive oil to the inner pot of the rice cooker and push the KEEP WARM button.

2. Heat the honey in a microwavable mixing bowl for 15 -25 seconds; add brown sugar and season salt to mixing bowl and combine well. Add ribs and toss to coat well.

3. Add ribs to the rice cooker.

4. Top with the barbecue sauce and very slowly pour beer into the rice cooker to keep from foaming over.

5. Lock lid into place and hit the PRESSURE COOK button until the rice cooker reads 25 minutes. When the timer goes off, add an additional 25 minutes.

6. Add the corn to the steamer basket and place into the rice cooker with the ribs. Lock the lid and press MEAT for 10 minutes.

7. Let ribs rest for five minutes after rice cooker goes off. Remove corn, then ribs, and plate with your other favorite sides.

Nutritional Info: Calories: 529, Sodium: 767 mg, Dietary Fiber: 2.3 g, Fat: 20.7 g, Carbs: 52 g, Protein: 24.9 g.

Dijon Chicken with Farro and Mushrooms

Decadent food has never been so good and so easy — especially when you can cook in half the time of a traditional meal. Whip up Dijon Chicken with Farro and Mushrooms on date night or when hosting friends on the weekend. Everyone will love this one pot meal that boasts of tantalizing flavors.

Servings 4

Cook Time 80 minutes

Ingredients

6 boneless chicken thighs, with the fat trimmed off

1 tsp. olive oil

2 shallots, minced

1 cup mushrooms, diced

1 cup farro

1 1/2 cups low-sodium chicken or vegetable broth

Marinade:

1 tsp. garlic powder

Pinch of nutmeg

1/3 cup balsamic vinegar

1 tsp. olive oil

1 tbsp. Dijon mustard

Pinch of sea salt

Pinch of ground black pepper

Instructions

1. Add all marinade ingredients to a plastic, resealable bag. Add chicken, turning to make sure each thigh is well-coated with marinade; refrigerate until needed.

2. Add 1 tsp. olive oil to the inner pot. Add shallots, stirring to coat, then lock lid. Hit the SAUTE button once and cook for 5 minutes, until shallots have softened.

3. Open rice cooker and add mushrooms. Hit the SAUTE button twice and cook 8 for minutes.

4. Open rice cooker and stir in farro and broth. Place chicken on top of farro mixture; discard any remaining marinade.

5. Lock the lid and press the POULTRY button until programmed for 30 minutes. Check the internal temperature of the chicken with a meat thermometer; if it does not read 165 degrees Fahrenheit—cook for additional 5-minute increments until the ideal temperature is reached.

6. Transfer portions to plates and serve hot with your favorite beverage.

Nutritional Info: Calories: 262, Sodium: 458 mg, Dietary Fiber: 2.1 g, Fat: 9.1 g, Carbs: 11.5 g, Protein: 32 g.

Shrimp with Lemon Risotto

Simple, fresh meals like Shrimp with Lemony Risotto can brighten up any dinner table. You'll love this bright Mediterranean style meal. Serve it with a cherry tomato salad and a glass of white wine.

Servings 4-6

Cook time 30 minutes

Ingredients

1 tbsp. olive oil

5 tsp. butter

1 cup onion, chopped fine

1/2 cup red bell pepper

1 tbsp. lemon zest

1 cup Arborio rice

1/4 cup white wine, like Sauvignon Blanc

3 cups chicken broth

24 medium shrimp, deveined, peeled and tailed

2 lemons, one juiced, one cut into wedges

1/2 cup parmesan cheese, grated

1/8 tsp. coarse black pepper

1 tbsp. Fresh parsley, chopped

Olive oil for drizzling

Instructions

1. Press the SAUTE button. When the bottom of the inner pot gets hot, add olive oil and butter.

2. Add onion and red bell pepper when butter is melted and sauté for about 3 minutes or until softened.

3. Stir in lemon zest.

4. Fold in rice until completely coated. Sauté for about 5 minutes or until mostly translucent.

5. Stir in wine and cook for 3 to 4 minutes or until evaporated. Stir in broth. Close the lid and push the STEAM button to 20 minutes; stir a few times while the risotto is cooking.

6.   Fold in shrimp and lemon juice. Set the STEAM button for 5 minutes. Shrimp should be pink and opaque; if risotto is too al dente cook for an additional 5 minutes.

7.   Fold in parmesan and black pepper.

8.   Serve garnished with parsley, lemon wedges, and an olive oil drizzle on top.

Nutritional Info: Calories: 237, Sodium: 454 mg, Dietary Fiber: 2.2 g, Fat: 7 g, Carbs: 32.9 g, Protein: 9.5 g.

Jambalaya

Bring home a taste of the Bayou with this delicious one-pot meal. Jambalaya is hearty, stick to your ribs dinner that is sure to become a favorite with your MultiPot. This comforting dish is delicious served with a glass of red wine or sparkling water.

Servings 5-6

Cook time 50 minutes

Ingredients

1/3 cup onion, diced

1 rib celery, very thinly sliced

1 tsp. olive oil

1/2 lb. andouille sausage, sliced

12 medium shrimp, deveined and peeled (optional)

1/2 cup French onion soup

1/2 cup low sodium chicken stock

2 (10 oz) cans diced tomatoes and green chilis like Rotel drained

1 (15 oz) can black-eyed peas, undrained

1 1/2 cups white or brown rice, uncooked

Instructions

1. Add olive oil to rice cooker and push SAUTE button.

2. Add onion and celery. Push SAUTE button to five minutes, lock lid and cook.

3. Open the rice cooker and add remaining ingredients. Stir to combine. Add 25 minutes using the STEAM button on the rice cooker.

4. Once finished, let it sit for 5 minutes; do not remove the lid.

5. Turn the rice cooker to STEAM for 10 additional minutes.

6. Stir and check rice to make sure it is done. If not, add a little more water (about 2 tbsp), stir, and set it to cook again for an additional five minutes.

7.   Serve with your favorite salad or on its own with a light beer or glass of lemonade.

Nutritional Info: Calories: 400, Sodium: 811 mg, Dietary Fiber: 5.1 g, Fat: 13.1 g, Carbs: 53.1 g, Protein: 17.3 g.

Pad Thai

With a hint of spice and a touch of sweet, you can whip up authentic Pad Thai right in the comfort of your own kitchen. This recipe combines authentic Thai ingredients that will have your taste buds craving more. A one-pot dish, Pad Thai is perfect served with hot or iced green tea!

Serving 4

Cook time 25 minutes

Ingredients

3/4 lb. chicken, cut into 2-inch strips

8 large shrimp deveined, peeled and tailed

8 oz. Thai Rice Noodles, medium #10

1/4 cup grapeseed oil

3 scallions, topped and thinly sliced

1 medium Carrot shaved into ribbons

1 cup Bean Sprouts

1 1/2 tsp. Fresh garlic, chopped

2 eggs

1 1/2 cups chicken broth

1/2 cup Unsalted Roasted Peanuts crushed, for garnish

1 lime cut into wedges, for garnish

Pad Thai Sauce

3 tbsp. tamarind paste

1/3 cup light brown sugar or brown sugar substitute

2 tbsp. fish sauce

1 tbsp. fresh lime juice

1 tbsp. tomato paste

1 tsp. ground chili paste, like Sambal Oelek

Instructions

1. Soak Noodles in hot water for 1-2 minutes and drain; noodles should bend slightly.

2. Add Pad Thai Sauce ingredients to a glass mixing bowl and whisk until well-blended.

3. Set pressure cooker to SAUTE for 5 minutes. Add olive oil, garlic, carrots, bean sprouts, and scallions to inner pot. Sauté for 1 minute.

4. Add chicken and sauté 1 minute.

5. Push ingredients to one side of the inner pot and crack eggs into the empty spot and scramble until almost firm. Fold into other ingredients.

6. Add broth. Fold in Pad Thai sauce and stir until well-combined.

7. Gently fold noodles into the sauce.

8. Lock lid in place and set to STEAM for 5 minutes.

9. Open the lid and lay shrimp on top of the Pad Thai. Replace lid and STEAM for 5 additional minutes. Place on KEEP WARM for 5 minutes.

10. Plate Pad Thai and serve garnished with peanuts and a lime wedge.

Nutritional Info: Calories: 642, Sodium: 781 mg, Dietary Fiber: 2.9 g, Fat: 29 g, Carbs: 49.6 g, Protein: 47.9 g.

Massaman Chicken

While traditional Massaman Chicken is cooked in clay pots, you can replicate the authentic taste of Thailand with this delicious one pot dish. Simple and easy, this recipe boasts of creamy coconut milk for a slightly sweet, comforting and savory meal. Great for lazy Sundays or cold days when you just need something to warm you up.

Servings 4

Cook time 1 hour 10 minutes

Ingredients

2/3 cups massaman curry paste

1 cup unsweetened coconut milk, from a can

4 chicken thighs, diced into 1-inch pieces

1/2 cup Belgian wheat beer

1/2 cup low sodium chicken broth

1 cup potato, chopped

1/2 cup onion, chopped

1 tbsp. tamarind paste

11/2 tbsp. palm sugar

2-3 bay leaves

1/4 cup roast cardamom

1/4 cup roast peanuts, chopped, for garnish

Instructions

1. Pour the coconut milk and massaman curry paste into the inner pot. Mix them thoroughly and lock the lid in place.

2. Set STEAM to 15 minutes and start. When the cycle is finished, add the rest of the ingredients to the inner pot and stir well to combine.

3. Set STEAM to 25 minutes for 2 cycles, and an additional 10-minute cycle; total cooking time 1 hour. Chicken should fall apart with the touch of a fork and be very tender.

4. Plate, top with roast peanuts, and enjoy!

Nutritional Info: Calories: 523, Sodium: 234 mg, Dietary Fiber: 3.4 g, Fat: 29.8 g, Carbs: 17.3 g, Protein: 48.6 g.

Balsamic Roast Beef with Rustic Vegetables

Serving 6-8

Cook time 1 hour 20 minutes

Ingredients

2 tsp. olive oil, divided

1 (2 1/2 lb.) boneless chuck roast

1/2 onion, sliced into 1-inch thick pieces

2 parsnips, diced thick

1 (15 oz) can diced tomatoes

1 cup beef broth

1/2 cup balsamic vinegar

1/2 cup red wine

1 tbsp. Worcestershire sauce

1/2 tsp. Garlic powder

1/2 teaspoon red pepper flakes

4 cloves garlic chopped

Instructions

1. Heat 1 tsp. olive oil in a large frying pan on high heat. Sear roast beef on each side for 3 minutes and transfer to the rice cooker.

2. Add an additional tablespoon of olive oil to the pan and turn to medium heat. Add onions and sauté 3 minutes.

3. Mix balsamic vinegar and wine together in a measuring cup and add to onions to caramelize for 5 minutes.

4. Transfer onions and juice to the rice cooker. Add remaining ingredients and lock the lid in place. Set the MEAT button for a total of 30 minutes. Leave on KEEP WARM for 10 additional minutes.

5. Remove roast from the inner pot, place on a cutting board, and slice. Spoon vegetables and au jus over plated roast to serve.

Nutritional Info: Calories: 314, Sodium: 196 mg, Dietary Fiber: 0.9 g, Fat: 15.4 g, Carbs: 4.3 g, Protein: 34.2 g.

Whole Roasted Chicken

Put your MultiPot Pressure Cooker to work and transform Sunday Brunch or a busy day with simple, healthy meals. You can cook a whole roasted chicken in a fraction of the time it takes to oven roast. You'll also save on added fat by roasting in the rice cooker! You can even use leftover chicken to quickly make soups and one pot dishes in the rice cooker to serve later in the week.

Serving 6-8

Cook time 1 hour 5 minutes

Ingredients

1 small chicken, up to 2 lbs.

1 tsp. sea salt

1 tsp. black pepper

1 tsp. chili powder

1 tsp. garlic powder

1 lemon

2 tsp. olive oil

2 shallots

1 rib of celery, sliced

Instructions

1. Mix sea salt, black pepper, chili powder, and garlic powder in a small mixing bowl; set aside.

2. Smash the shallots with the flat side of a knife, on a cutting board, to break each into two or three pieces.

3. Cut the lemon into thin slices, then cut slices in half. Slide your fingers under the top skin of the chicken and pull it up, place lemon slices under the skin, and stretch it back over to cover the lemon slices.

4. Heat 1 tsp. olive oil in a frying pan over medium-high heat. Sear the chicken on each side for about 5-8 minutes, or until the skin has darkened and is a little crispy.

5. Rub chicken with the remaining teaspoon of olive oil, and coat oiled chicken with seasoning mix.

6.   Shove remaining lemon and shallots into the chicken cavity.

7.   Set POULTRY button for 1 hour.

8.   Chicken is ready to serve when juices run clear, and meat is no longer pink.

Nutritional Info: Calories: 23, Sodium: 243 mg, Dietary Fiber: 0.4 g, Fat: 1.4 g, Carbs: 1.6 g, Protein: 1.6 g.

Pineapple Chicken Fajitas

Chicken Fajitas are fun for the whole family, especially when cooked in your MultiPot. This is a great one-pot meal to use the delay time and start while you are on your way home. Simply prepare the meal, set the timer for the desired delay and finish cooking when you get home.

Servings 4

Cook time 1 hour 10 minutes

Ingredients

1 lb. chicken thighs

2 bell peppers, any color, sliced thin

1 cup pineapple chunks, drained if using canned

1/2 medium onion, sliced thin

2 cloves garlic

1 tbsp. tomato paste

1 cup chicken broth

1 tsp. chili powder

1 tsp. cumin

1/4 tsp. oregano

1/2 tsp. paprika

1/2 tsp. garlic powder

1/2 teaspoon sea salt

1/4 teaspoon freshly ground black pepper

1 (15 oz.) can black beans, drained

1 tsp. hot sauce

6 corn tortillas

1 avocado, sliced for garnish

1/2 cup sour cream, for garnish

Cotija cheese, for garnish

Instructions

1. Mix the tomato paste, chicken broth, and spices in a small mixing bowl.

2. Add bell peppers, onion, chicken, pineapple, and seasoning mix to inner pot of rice cooker.

3. Close lid and set POULTRY for 40 minutes total. Remove chicken and set aside.

4. Add the black beans and hot sauce. Set STEAM for an additional 15 minutes, or until the liquid has reduced.

5. Shred the chicken while the vegetables are cooking. When 15 minutes is up, fold the chicken back into the inner pot of the rice cooker and press KEEP WARM for five minutes to warm the chicken.

6. Serve on corn tortillas with avocado, sour cream, and cotija cheese.

Nutritional Info: Calories: 623, Sodium: 995 mg, Dietary Fiber: 12.9 g, Fat: 26.5 g, Carbs: 54.3 g, Protein: 45.2 g.

One Pot Teriyaki Chicken and Vegetables

Everyone loves a quick and easy dinner! Whip up this healthy One Pot Teriyaki Chicken and Vegetables for a tantalizing, yet healthy meal. Serve in bowls while hot with green tea or plum wine for an authentically Asian restaurant style night in.

Servings 3-4

Cook time 30 minutes

Ingredients

1 1/2 tbsp. sesame oil

1 medium boneless skinless chicken breast, cut into cubes

Sea salt

Black pepper

2 cloves garlic, minced

1/2 tsp. minced ginger

1/3 cup red bell peppers, chopped

1/3 cup carrot, shredded

1 1/2 cups Jasmine rice, rinsed and drained thoroughly

1 cup water

1 cup broccoli florets

1/3 cup frozen shelled Edamame beans, thawed

Sesame seeds, for garnish

Teriyaki Sauce:

1/3 cup soy sauce

1/4 cup rice wine vinegar

1/4 cup honey

1 1/2 tbsp. Mirin

1 tsp. cornstarch

3 tbsp. water, plus more as needed to thin out the sauce

Instructions

1. Preheat rice cooker on SAUTE for 5 minutes.

2. Whisk soy sauce, vinegar, honey, mirin and starch in a mixing bowl. Pour into a saucepan and heat on medium high heat. Slowly add water and bring to a boil, until thickened; transfer to a heat-safe bowl.

62

3. Add sesame oil to inner pot and SAUTE for 1 minute.

4. Add the chicken and season with sea salt and pepper when oil is hot. Saute for 2 minutes, until golden brown.

5. Add the garlic and ginger and cook for another 20 seconds.

6. Fold in 1/2 cup of the teriyaki sauce, rice, bell peppers, carrots, broccoli, edamame, and water; STEAM for 10 minutes or until vegetables are tender.

7. Drizzle with additional teriyaki sauce, top with sesame seeds, and serve.

Nutritional Info: Calories: 463, Sodium: 273 mg, Dietary Fiber: 6.3 g, Fat: 7.4 g, Carbs: 83.9 g, Protein: 14.3 g.

Vegetarian Portobello Pot Roast

Vegetarian Portobello Pot Roast is the perfect comfort food for cool fall days or cold winter nights. Hearty and rich, this pot roast will have your taste buds craving more. Perfect on its own or served with buttered egg noodles, this dish is sure to warm your soul and your foodie loving heart.

Servings 6-8

Cook time 1 hour 10 minutes

Ingredients

1 pound portobello mushrooms, cut into two inch pieces

2 large carrots, peeled and diced

3 large parsnips, diced large

1 rib of celery, chopped

1 cup frozen pearl onions

4 cloves garlic, peeled and minced

3 sprigs fresh thyme

3 cups vegetable stock, divided

1/2 cup dry red wine

3 tbsp. tomato paste

2 tbsp. Vegetarian Worcestershire sauce

2 tbsp. cornstarch

Kosher salt and freshly-cracked black pepper

Egg noodles with butter, optional side

Instructions

1. Add mushrooms, carrots, parsnips, celery, onions, garlic, thyme, 2 1/2 cups vegetable stock, wine and Worcestershire to the inner pot of the rice cooker; gently toss to combine.

2. Lock lid in place and STEAM for a total of one hour.

3. Whisk together the remaining 1/2 cup vegetable stock and cornstarch until well-combined. Add to the pot roast and gently toss to combine.

4.   Continue on STEAM for an additional 5 minutes, until the sauce thickens.

5.   Serve hot and enjoy with buttered egg noodles!

Nutritional Info: Calories: 78, Sodium: 331 mg, Dietary Fiber: 2.7 g, Fat: 0.2 g, Carbs: 14.8 g, Protein: 2.4 g.

Hawaiian Fried Rice

Cook your family a sweet and savory meal, even the kids will love this delicious Hawaiian Fried Rice recipe. While this recipe calls for ham, you can sub out with tofu for a delicious Vegetarian twist. Serve this delicious dish with your favorite side salad for one scrumptious, healthy meal.

Serving 6

Cook time 50 minutes

Ingredients

2 tsp. sesame oil

1/2 tsp. garlic powder

1 small onion, diced

1 red bell pepper, diced

2 cups ham, cooked and chopped into 1/2 -inch cubes

3 eggs

1 1/2 cups brown rice, uncooked and rinsed

2 cups water

2 tbsp. soy sauce

1 cup pineapple, diced

1 scallion, sliced thin for garnish

Instructions

1. Add the sesame oil to the inner pot and press STEAM for five minutes. Heat oil for 2 minutes, then adds the onion and red pepper to saute for remaining 3 minutes. Stir and saute for 5 additional minutes or until softened.

2. Add the ham to the rice cooker and saute for 5 minutes.

3. Beat eggs in a small mixing bowl until well-combined. Push the ham mixture to one side and add the eggs and scramble until firm and cooked through.

4. Add remaining ingredients, stir to combine, lock the lid in place, and set to STEAM for 25 minutes.

5. Leave Hawaiian Fried Rice on KEEP WARM for 10 minutes. Divide the rice into bowls and garnish with scallions to serve.

Nutritional Info: Calories: 319, Sodium: 924 mg, Dietary Fiber: 3.2 g, Fat: 8.9 g, Carbs: 45 g, Protein: 14.7 g.

General Tso's Chicken

This Asian style restaurant favorite with a twist is one healthy way to curb cravings when it comes to clean eating. Whip up General Tso's Chicken and serve in lettuce cups or with a side of steamed vegetables and brown rice. No matter which way you love to serve this classic dish, you're taste buds will fall in love with this recipe.

Serving 2-4

Cook time 45 minutes

Ingredients

3 garlic cloves, minced

1 tsp. fresh ginger, roughly chopped

1 tbsp. grapeseed oil

10 dried Chinese red chili

5 boneless skinless chicken thighs

1 stalk green onion, green part finely chopped for garnish, white part cut into 1.5-inch pieces

1 tbsp. honey

8-10 pieces of bibb lettuce or romaine

General Tso's Sauce:

1/4 cup dark soy sauce

2 tbsp. Shaoxing rice wine

2 tbsp. distilled white vinegar

1/3 cup sugar or sugar substitute

1 tsp. sesame oil

Thickening agent

2 tbsp. cornstarch

2 tbsp. water

Instructions

1. Whisk together the General Tso's Sauce ingredients in a glass mixing bowl until well-combined and set aside.

2. Add grapeseed oil to rice cooker and add 5 minutes to SAUTE. Add garlic and ginger after 2 minutes. Saute until translucent and softened; about 3 minutes.

3. Add dried Chinese red chili, the whites of the green onions. Cook for 3 minutes until fragrant.

4. Add sauce and chicken thighs to the inner pot. Close lid and set POULTRY for 25 minutes.

5. Remove the chicken from the inner pot and shred with a fork.

6. Remove the Chinese red chili. Add honey and bring the sauce back to a boil on STEAM.

7. Mix the cornstarch and water for the thickening agent in a small mixing bowl. Fold into the sauce one third at a time until desired thickness.

8. Fold shredded chicken into the sauce and replace the lid on KEEP WARM for 5 minutes.

9. Assemble lettuce leaves on a plate. Spoon in the desired amount of General Tso's Chicken and garnish with green onion to serve.

Nutritional Info: Calories: 727, Sodium: 637 mg, Dietary Fiber: 1.3 g, Fat: 21.9 g, Carbs: 73.9 g, Protein: 69.4 g.

Super-Easy Spanish Paella

Paella is a traditional dish from Spain sure to turn dinner into something out of this world. This recipe combines delicious complex flavors and helps you put something amazing on the table in no time. Substitute meats for soy-rizo, jackfruit, and mushrooms and you've got one tantalizing vegetarian paella.

Servings 6

Cook time 40 minutes

Ingredients

2 tbsp. olive oil, divided

1 yellow onion, diced

1 red bell pepper, diced

1 green bell pepper, diced

2 cloves garlic, minced

2 tsp. smoked paprika

2 tsp. dried oregano

1 pinch saffron

3/4 tsp. sea salt

1/2 tsp. crushed red pepper flakes

Coarse ground black pepper

1 bay leaf

1 (15 oz.) can diced tomatoes

3 cups low-sodium vegetable or chicken broth

11/2 cups brown rice

3 boneless skinless chicken thighs, cut into 1-inch pieces

12 large shrimp or tiger prawns, deveined and peeled

1/4 cup chorizo

1/2 cup frozen peas, defrosted

1/4 cup sliced black olives

Hot sauce, for garnish

Freshly chopped parsley, for garnish

Instructions

1.   Heat 1 tablespoon olive oil in the rice cooker on SAUTE for 3 minutes.

2.   Add onion and bell peppers. Cook until soft, about 7 minutes.

3.   Add garlic to rice cooker and sauté for 1 minute or until fragrant.

4.   Add the broth, then fold in smoked paprika, oregano, sea salt, crushed red pepper, black pepper, bay leaf, diced tomatoes with liquid, and rice. Press MULTIGRAIN button and cook through the cycle.

5.   Heat remaining olive oil in a frying pan over medium-high heat. Add chicken thighs and chorizo. Cook until browned and no pink shows in the chicken; about 10 to 12 minutes. Fold cooked chicken and sausage into the rice.

6.   Add saffron, peas, and black olives to the rice cooker.

7.   STEAM for 5 minutes to combine flavors.

8.   Serve garnished with hot sauce and chopped parsley.

Nutritional Info: Calories: 371, Sodium: 788 mg, Dietary Fiber: 4.7 g, Fat: 13.3 g, Carbs: 31.9 g, Protein: 30.8 g.

Rice Cooker Mahi Mahi

Whip up one tantalizing main meal with a delicious heart-healthy Mediterranean style Mahi Mahi. This delicious dish is simple and easy and great for cooking on busy days. Forget the oven, you can cook delicious, diet-friendly, gourmet style meals in no time with your MultiPot.

Serving 4-6

Cooking Time 20 minutes

Ingredients

3 lb. mahi-mahi fish fillets

Coarse sea salt

White Pepper

2 lemons, 1 juiced, 1 cut into wedges

2 tsp. Olive oil

Garnish: lemon wedges and olive oil

Instructions

1. Rinse fish with cold water and pat dry with a paper towel. Rub with olive oil, sea salt, and white pepper.

2. Add 2 cups of water to the inner pot.

3. Place fish in the steam tray and drizzle evenly with lemon juice.

4. Place the steam tray in the rice cooker. Lock lid and steam for 15 minutes or until cooked through; meat should be tender and cooked white through.

5. Transfer onto plates and garnish with additional lemon juice and olive oil.

Nutritional Info: Calories: 188, Sodium: 264 mg, Dietary Fiber: 0.8 g, Fat: 3.3 g, Carbs: 4.3 g, Protein: 35.2 g.

Honey Bourbon Chicken

Whip up an easy to make meal any night of the week with Honey Bourbon Chicken. Healthy and scrumptious, this meal is bursting with flavors that will have everyone wanting seconds. Serve with steamed vegetables or a side salad for one healthy meal when you don't have a lot of time to cook during your busy schedule.

Servings 4

Cook Time 20 minutes

Ingredients

4-5 boneless skinless chicken thighs

1/2 tsp. garlic powder

2 tsp. ground chili paste, like Sambal Oelek

3/4 cups ketchup

3/4 cups honey

1/4 cup bourbon, like Maker's Mark

2 tbsp. potato starch

1 bag frozen broccoli, thawed

Instructions

1. Add water, ketchup, honey, bourbon, chili paste, and garlic to the inner pot and stir to combine.

2. Fold in chicken and coat well.

3. Lock lid and press STEAM for 10 minutes.

4. Remove some sauce and transfer to a glass measuring cup. Whisk in potato starch until dissolved. Fold into the inner pot with chicken.

5. Place broccoli in the steam tray and place in the rice cooker. Replace lid and STEAM for an additional 10 minutes.

6. Plate together and enjoy!

Nutritional Info: Calories: 363, Sodium: 617 mg, Dietary Fiber: 0.9 g, Fat: 2.5 g, Carbs: 70.5 g, Protein: 12.7 g.

6

**RICE RECIPES
(White/Brown/Basmati/Multi-
Grain...etc.)**

The Perfect Sushi Rice

Delicious, perfect sushi rice has never been so easy! Sushi rice is great for hosting sushi parties with friends or meal prepping sushi lunches to go for the whole family. Whether you love creating California Rolls, Cucumber Rolls or decadent Soy Paper Hand Rolls – this Sushi Rice is absolutely delicious and diet friendly.

Servings 8

Cook time 30 minutes

Ingredients

4 cups short grain/sushi rice

Water

Su for Sushi Rice

1 cup rice wine vinegar

1/2 cup sugar

1/4 cup mirin

Ingredients

1. Add rice to the inner pot. Fill with water to line 4. Set RICE to 27 minutes.

2. Heat vinegar, sugar, and mirin in a saucepan until sugar is dissolved; let cool to room temperature.

3. Gently fold the Su into the rice.

4. Let rice stand for 10 minutes and fold again.

5. Use the sushi rice to create your favorite sushi or host a sushi building party!

Nutritional Info: Calories: 437, Sodium: 66 mg, Dietary Fiber: 2.8 g, Fat: 0.5 g, Carbs: 95.2 g, Protein: 6.5 g.

Rice Cooker Pasta

When you need to save time in the kitchen, this Rice Cooker Pasta Recipe is the way to go. Simple and easy, you can press a button on this dish and walk away. While the recipe isn't all that decadent, you can add any sauce, cheese, or meat and really spice things up in your MultiPot Pressure Cooker on a busy day or night.

Servings 3

Cook time 25 minutes

Ingredients

2 cups uncooked pasta

2 cups water

1/4 tsp. sea salt

1 tsp. olive oil

1 cup favorite sauce, or 4 tsp. Butter, optional

1/2 tsp. garlic powder, optional

parmesan cheese, for topping

Instructions

1. Place water, pasta, sea salt and olive oil in the inner pot of the rice cooker, and gently stir to combine. Here, you can also add your favorite sauce or butter, and garlic powder.

2. Close lid and press RICE; stir once or twice during the cycle to keep from sticking together.

3. Do not leave on warm to keep from browning or caking together. You can pan fry meat like ground round or chicken to add in at the beginning of the cooking process.

4. Serve with your favorite sauce, veggies, meat, or enjoy on its own with butter and cheese!

Nutritional Info: Calories: 261, Sodium: 183 mg, Dietary Fiber: 0.1 g, Fat: 3.5 g, Carbs: 47 g, Protein: 9.7 g.

Spanish Rice

Spanish Rice is the perfect Mexican or South Western side dish. Of course, you can also add your favorite lean meats or a fish and really kick things up a notch when it comes to healthy eating. Press a button and walk away dish, this quick and easy recipe will really help you transform dinner in no time.

Servings 4-5

Cook time 35 minutes

Ingredients

2 cups rice

1 tsp. olive oil

1 (14 oz.) can diced tomatoes

3 1/2 cups water

1 small yellow onion, diced

3 chicken or vegetable bouillon cubes

2 tbsp. chili powder

1 tsp. cumin

1/2 tsp. sea salt

1/2 tsp. garlic powder

Instructions

1. Combine rice, water, and diced tomatoes in the inner pot.

2. Fold in the onion, bouillon cubes and spices into the rice and stir well to help the spices dissolve in the water.

3. Press the RICE button.

4. Keep warm until serving with your favorite lean meats, enchiladas, or tacos! Alternatively, you can use the rice to fill burritos for an authentic South Western meal.

Nutritional Info: Calories: 468, Sodium: 502 mg, Dietary Fiber: 4 g, Fat: 11.6 g, Carbs: 74.6 g, Protein: 15.5 g.

Brown Rice

Brown Rice has become a star in the eyes of clean eating over the last few years, and we've got the perfect way to whip it up quick. Traditional Brown Rice cooking methods can take a very long time, but when you put it in the MultiPot Pressure Cooker- you can press one button, walk away, and done.

Servings 2

Cook time

Ingredients

2 cups brown rice   *Salt to taste*

Water

Instructions

1. Add brown rice to the inner pot of the rice cooker.

2. Add water 2 1/2 cups water.

3. Add a pinch or two of salt to taste.

4. Stir, lock lid in place, and press the RICE button.

5. Fluff with a fork and serve with your favorite meals!

Nutritional Info: Calories: 0, Sodium: 0 mg, Dietary Fiber: 0 g, Fat: 0 g, Carbs: 0 g, Protein: 0 g.

Multigrain Rice

Multigrain Rice used to take what seemed like days to cook, but with your MultiPot you can whip up a healthy multi-grain meal in no time. The best part about cooking Multigrain Rice in your cooker is the many delicious combinations you can choose to explore.

Servings 8

Cook time 45-55 minutes

Ingredients

2 cups rice

4 cups water

1 - 2 cups of any grain on the list below:

(Keep in mind: your rice cooker only holds 4 cups of grains, so do not overfill.)

Brown rice

Sweet brown rice

White rice

Wild rice

Red rice

Pearl barley

Steel cut oats

Amaranth

Sorghum

Millet

Black rice

Farro

Buckwheat

Quinoa

Black-eye peas

Soy Beans

Split peas

Garbanzo beans

Kidney beans

Mung beans

Sesame seeds

Instructions

1. Combine your choice of grains and rice in a large mixing bowl. Gently rinse the rice mixture twice in cold water; drain the water as much as possible without losing the grains in the sink.

2. Add the multigrain rice to the rice cooker and fill with 4 cups of water. Press the MULTIGRAIN button.

3. KEEP WARM for 10 minutes, fluff multigrain rice and serve. You can store the leftover rice in a freezer bag for future use; to thaw, microwave your desired amount on high for 2-3 minutes.

Nutritional Info: Calories: 341, Sodium: 8 mg, Dietary Fiber: 2.2 g, Fat: 1.6 g, Carbs: 73.2 g, Protein: 6.9 g.

Cauliflower Rice

Cauliflower Rice is even more simple and easy to make in your MultiPot. This delicious rice substitute is perfect for those who follow Paleo, Gluten-Free, or just want to cut carbohydrates. Don't be afraid to dress it up with a packet of ranch seasoning or toss it in buffalo sauce for a savory twist on this delicious dish.

Servings 4

Cook time 25 minutes

Ingredients

1 head of cauliflower

2 tsp. olive oil

1/4 tsp. sea salt

1/8 tsp. white pepper

Instructions

1. Rinse the cauliflower and trim off the leaves. Cut cauliflower into 5 to 7 large pieces.

2. Add 1 cup of water to the inner pot, then add cauliflower. Lock the lid and set STEAM for 5 minutes.

3. Remove the cauliflower to a cutting board. Discard the water in the rice cooker.

4. Add the olive oil to the inner pot and cooked cauliflower. Break up with a potato masher or wooden spoon.

5. Add sea salt and white pepper; stir to combine well. Replace lid, lock, and set to STEAM for 20 minutes.

6. Enjoy with your favorite dishes for a grain-free alternative. Alternatively, for an Asian inspired meal—swap the olive oil for sesame oil.

Nutritional Info: Calories: 18, Sodium: 68 mg, Dietary Fiber: 0.8 g, Fat: 1.2 g, Carbs: 1.8 g, Protein: 0.7 g.

Vegetable Rice

Whip up a side or main meal of Vegetable Rice in no time with this yummy recipe. Transform plain Jasmine rice into a healthy treat with vegetables for a quick one-pot meal. Enjoy this dish with your favorite meat or tofu for a scrumptious family meal.

Servings 4

Cook time 30 minutes

INGREDIENTS:

2 cups Jasmine rice

1 small carrot, finely chopped

1/4 cup white cabbage, shredded

1/2 small onion, finely chopped

1/3 cup green beans, chopped small

8 button mushrooms, chopped small

3 tbsp. soy sauce, extra for drizzling

2 tbsp. sake

1 1/2 tbsp. mirin

1/2 tsp. sea salt

3 scallions, finely chopped

Instructions

1. Add rice to the inner pot and rinse until water runs clear; drain.

2. Place inner pot in the rice cooker. Add soy sauce, sake, mirin, and salt and add water up to the FILL LINE 2, measuring line, in the pot.

3. Top with carrots, cabbage, onion, green beans, and mushrooms; do not stir.

4. Lock the lid in place and set the rice cooker to RICE.

5. Gently fluff the rice with a fork and serve hot topped with scallions and extra soy sauce!

Nutritional Info: Calories: 385, Sodium: 973 mg, Dietary Fiber: 5.7 g, Fat: 0.1 g, Carbs: 86 g, Protein: 8.5 g.

No Fuss Beans

Beans are a great way to add extra fiber to your diet and supplement grains in healthy recipes. This recipe helps you cook them for a quarter of the time. No more watching the pot all day, you can create a pot of savory beans in a quarter of the time.

Servings 3

Cook time 25 hours 30 minutes

Ingredients

2 cup dried beans, like pinto, navy or black beans

1 bay leaf

1 small ham hock, optional (for vegetarian add 1 vegetable bouillon cube)

Water

Chopped onion, optional

Black pepper, optional

Sea salt, optional

Instructions

1. Add beans to the inner pot and cover with water; soak overnight.

2. Drain and rinse the beans, the following morning, put them back in the rice cooker, and add 4 cups of water, along with 1 bay leaf and a ham hock or bouillon cube.

3. Turn the rice cooker to BEANS and cook for one hour.

4. Check that beans are still covered with water after the cycle; if needed, add a little more water and set BEANS cycle for an additional 30 minutes.

5. Remove the bay leaf and ham hock. Serve beans hot as a soup with chopped onion, sea salt, and pepper — or drain and use in your favorite recipes.

Nutritional Info: Calories: 148, Sodium: 38 mg, Dietary Fiber: 2.7 g, Fat: 8.8 g, Carbs: 5.7 g, Protein: 11.7 g.

Basmati Rice

Basmati Rice is an absolutely delicious way to add fluffy, season grains to any meal. Whip up a traditional Biryani or serve alongside your favorite curry for a hearty and healthy meal. Basmati Rice can also be used to add texture and flavor to soups when seasoned with bay leaves.

Servings 4

Cook time 40 minutes

Ingredients

2 cups Basmati Rice

Water

Pinch of sea salt

1 tsp. olive oil

Cardamom pods, optional

Bay leaf, optional

Instructions

1. Add rice to a large mixing bowl. Cover with water and let soak for 30 minutes.

2. Drain rice and rinse, with tap water, until water runs clear.

3. Rinse the rice. Run tap water in the bowl.

4. Pour rice into rice cooker and add 1 cup of water per 1 cup of rice.

5. Add sea salt and olive oil, as well as optional seasonings like Cardamom or Bay Leaf.

6. Lock lid in place, press the RICE button; when cooking cycle stops, leave on KEEP WARM for 10 minutes and serve!

Nutritional Info: Calories: 348, Sodium: 63 mg, Dietary Fiber: 1.2 g, Fat: 1.8 g, Carbs: 74 g, Protein: 6.6 g.

Quick and Easy Lentils

Gone are the days when lentils took days to cook. Lentils are delicious served alongside roasted vegetables and sliced avocado. Lentils also make the perfect addition to your favorite soups for a hearty punch.

Servings

Cook time 1 hour 10 minutes

Ingredients

1 cup lentils

Water

1 tbsp. olive oil

1/4 tsp. sea salt

1/8 tsp. coarse black pepper

Ingredients

1. Pour lentils into a colander and rinse with cold water.

2. Add the lentils to the rice cooker, top with 2 cups of water; stir to combine.

3. Fold in olive oil, sea salt, and black pepper.

4. Lock lid into place, press MULTIGRAIN, and cook one hour. Leave on KEEP WARM for 10 minutes after the cycle is finished.

5. Transfer the lentils to a bowl and serve.

Nutritional Info: Calories: 0, Sodium: 0 mg, Dietary Fiber: 0 g, Fat: 0 g, Carbs: 0 g, Protein: 0 g.

7

VEGETABLE AND SIDE DISH
RECIPES

Steamed Broccoli

Steamed broccoli is a delicious way to complete any healthy meal. Hearty with an earthy taste broccoli, can be brightened up with a touch of sea salt and lemon juice for an even healthier twist. Pack your diet with extra fiber and create a delicious side in minutes with this recipe.

Ingredients

1 head of broccoli

2 cups of water

Sea salt, garnish

Lemon wedges, garnish

Olive oil, optional garnish

Instructions

1. Cut the florets off the broccoli and discard the stalk (or reserve for another use).

2. Pour 2 cups of water into rice cooker pot.

3. Rinse florets in running water and place in steam basket. Place basket in the rice cooker and close lid.

4. Using the STEAM COOK feature, steam broccoli for 3 minutes; don't leave on 'keep warm' or broccoli will wilt.

5. Remove broccoli, plate with your favorite meal. Garnish with sea salt, lemon juice and a drizzle of olive oil.

Nutritional Info: Calories: 0, Sodium: 0 mg, Dietary Fiber: 0 g, Fat: 0 g, Carbs: 0 g, Protein: 0 g.

Quinoa and Pomegranate Salad

Delightful and bright this salad is sure to be the star of any meal. A delicious meal for vegetarians, you can also jazz this recipe up with canned chicken or tuna. Simply drain and drizzle with lemon juice and pepper, and you'll have one seriously protein packed healthy option.

Ingredients

2 cups quinoa, rinsed

4 cups water

pinch of sea salt

1/2 lemon, juiced

2 tsp. olive oil

1/8 tsp. Coarse ground black pepper

1 tsp. honey

1 tsp. balsamic vinegar

1 cup pomegranate seeds

1/2 cup chopped fresh mint

Manchego cheese, chopped, optional garnish

Instructions

1. Add quinoa, water, and a pinch of salt to the MultiPot cooker. Lock lid in place and press RICE.

2. Open the lid and transfer quinoa to a large mixing bowl.

3. Add everything except mint and cheese; stir well to combine.

4. Gently fold in mint and cheese and enjoy!

Nutritional Info: Calories: 744, Sodium: 148 mg, Dietary Fiber: 14.1 g, Fat: 15.2 g, Carbs: 128.1 g, Protein: 25.4g.

Cuban Black Beans and Rice

A taste of Cuba is simple and easy when you create this delicious dish using your MultiPot. Enjoy these delicious black beans on their own or use as a tasty filling for burritos or salad bowls! Served in lettuce cups with salsa and avocado they make for a tantalizing vegetarian meal.

Servings 4-6

Cook time 1 hour 10 minutes

Ingredients

2 cups black beans, dry

4 cups water

1 small onion, chopped

1 small green bell pepper, chopped

1 clove garlic, minced

1 tsp. olive oil

1 tsp. cumin

1/4 tsp. oregano

1/4 tsp. garlic powder

1/4 tsp. sugar or sugar substitute

1 bay leaf

1/3 cup white wine

Olive oil, for garnish

Instructions

1. Add black beans to the inner pot and cover with water; soak overnight. Drain and rinse the beans, the next morning put them back in the rice cooker, and add 4 cups of water, along with 1 bay leaf.

2. Turn the rice cooker to RICE and cook for 30 minutes. Add one teaspoon of olive oil to a frying pan. Add onion and green pepper. Cook until translucent; about 5-7 minutes. Add garlic and cook for 1 minute longer.

3. After beans are finished cooking, fold in the onion mixture, seasoning, sugar, and white wine. Add RICE cycle for the second time. Serve beans hot over RICE and enjoy!

Nutritional Info: Calories: 253, Sodium: 10 mg, Dietary Fiber: 10.5 g, Fat: 1.9 g, Carbs: 44.1 g, Protein: 14.5 g.

Cheesy Polenta

Ooey gooey, cheesy polenta is a comforting side dish without the gluten. A great substitute for traditional grains and pasta, polenta is also delicious topped with roasted vegetables and olive oil. When you want to whip up something different to dine on this recipe is out of this world.

Servings 4

Cook time 40 minutes

Ingredients

2 tbsp. butter

1/2 sweet onion, chopped

1 shallot, minced

1 cup chicken broth

1 cup milk

1/2 cup polenta

1/4 tsp. sea salt, or more to taste

1/4 cup mozzarella cheese, shredded

1/4 cup parmesan cheese, shaved

Instructions

1. Add butter, onion, and shallot to rice cooker inner pot; lock the lid in place and cook on RICE until onion is soft and translucent, stirring occasionally 10 to 15 minutes.

2. Add chicken broth, milk, polenta, and sea salt. Replace lid and cook on RICE, for 20 minutes until polenta has absorbed the liquid; stir occasionally.

3. Fold in the cheese and stir until melted. Serve hot and enjoy!

Nutritional Info: Calories: 178, Sodium: 406 mg, Dietary Fiber: 0.8 g, Fat: 8.2 g, Carbs: 20.3 g, Protein: 6 g.

Cheesy Jalapeno Bread

Whip up some delicious cheesy jalapeno bread to serve with your favorite soups and salads. A fan favorite for football season, this bread is great when served with even pepperoni or cold cuts for homemade sandwiches or tailgate snacks.

Servings 4-6

Cook time 2 hours 45 minutes

Ingredients

2 1/2 cups bread flour

1 tsp. yeast

1 1/2 tbsp. sugar, plus one pinch

1 1/2 tsp. salt

1 1/2 tbsp. butter

2 tbsp. milk

3/4 cups water

3/4 cups pickled jalapenos, chopped

1/2 cups white cheddar cheese, shredded

Instructions

1. Add yeast to a large mixing bowl. Fold in a pinch of sugar and about 1/4 cup warm water; set aside for 10 minutes while yeast activates. When activated yeast will look foamy.

2. Add flour, salt, and sugar into the inner pot of the rice cooker and stir to combine.

3. Fold the milk and then the yeast into inner pot. Use hands to mix and form a dough ball.

4. Stick the butter in the middle of the dough ball. Add jalapenos and knead for 10 minutes until butter and jalapenos are incorporated.

5. Form the dough back into a ball and place in the inner pot of the rice cooker to rise for 30 minutes, if it rises too much it will stick to the top of the rice cooker.

6. When the dough has risen, use your hand to form it into a ball again, then let it rise for an additional hour.

7.   Press RICE and cook for one hour. After one hour, flip the bread, sprinkle with cheddar cheese and cook for an additional 45 minutes to 1 hour.

Nutritional Info: Calories: 269, Sodium: 665 mg, Dietary Fiber: 1.6 g, Fat: 6.6 g, Carbs: 43.4 g, Protein: 8.2 g.

Rice Cooker Bread

Rice Cooker Bread is a delicious way to serve up something hearty and special. If you don't buy bread all that often this is a great recipe to bake just enough for a nice treat. If you love bread, then this recipe will quench your appetite for home cooked, warm bread right out of the oven.

Servings 8-10

Cook time 29 hours

Ingredients

3 cups all-purpose or bread flour, additional flour for dusting

1/4 tsp. instant yeast

1 1/4 tsp. salt

1 1/2 cups water

Ingredients

1. Combine the dry ingredients in the rice cooker and fold in 1 1/2 cups of water until well-combined.

2. Leave the dough to rise in an unplugged rice cooker 12-18 hours; do not let rise for more than 18 hours as the dough will break down and not bake. You will know it is ready when the bubbles appear on the surface.

3. Dust the top of the dough with flour, then flour your hands. Fold the dough over onto itself twice. Use your hands to tuck the dough under itself to form a round loaf.

4. Leave to rise for an additional 2 hours. Press the RICE button.

5. Gently lift the bread up flip it over. Press the RICE button; flip for a second time on each side for a total cook time of 2 hours.

6. Bread is ready when slightly golden on both sides. You can brown the crust even further by finishing the loaf in the oven at 450 degrees Fahrenheit for 10-15 minutes.

Nutritional Info: Calories: 149, Sodium: 293 mg, Dietary Fiber: 1 g, Fat: 0.7 g, Carbs: 29.9 g, Protein: 5 g.

Steamed Artichokes

Serving 2

Cook Time 30 minutes

Steamed artichokes are a delicious delicacy when they are in season. A healthy side dish, you can also chop artichokes to elevate and pasta puttanesca. Serve with grilled white fish or pork loin for one tantalizing meal.

Ingredients

2 whole artichokes

2 lemons, cut into wedges

olive oil, for drizzling

sea salt, to serve

Instructions

1. Cut a third of the top off an artichoke. Trim the stem off as well as any thorny tips from the outer leaves.

2. Rub lemon wedges over the cut edges to prevent browning.

3. Add 3/4 cup of water to the inner pot of the rice cooker.

4. Add the artichoke to the steamer basket, place in steamer, lock lid into place. STEAM for 20 to 30 minutes, or until leaves pull off easily.

5. Remove from rice steamer, drizzle with olive oil and a dash of sea salt to serve.

Nutritional Info: Calories: 85, Sodium: 122 mg, Dietary Fiber: 9.3 g, Fat: 0.4 g, Carbs: 21.3 g, Protein: 5.1 g.

Mediterranean Quinoa Salad with Red Wine Vinaigrette

If you love quinoa, you'll fall head over heels for this rice cooker recipe. This delicious dish is served best with Mahi Mahi or Grilled Halloumi for one tantalizing Mediterranean treat. Serve with sparkling water and cucumber to really bring out the essence of this amazing side dish.

Servings 6

Cook time 40 minutes

Ingredients

1/2 cup quinoa

2/3 cups water

1/2 cups onion, chopped

1/2 cups cucumbers, diced

1/2 cups black cherries, diced

1/2 cups cherry tomatoes, chopped

1/2 cup buffalo mozzarella, coarsely chopped

For the vinaigrette:

2 tbsp. olive oil

1 tbsp. red wine, like Chianti

1 tbsp. balsamic vinegar

1/2 tsp. garlic powder

1/8 tsp. sugar or sugar substitute

1 dash sea salt, to taste

Instructions

1. Rinse quinoa under cold running water for a few seconds, until water runs clear.

2. Add quinoa and water to the inner pot rice cooker and press FLASH RICE.

3. Add vinaigrette ingredients to a small mixing bowl and whisk until well-combined.

4.   Fluff the quinoa with a fork and transfer to a large mixing bowl; let cool for about 5 minutes.

5.   Fold in the vegetables and cheese.

6.   Pour the red wine vinaigrette over the salad and toss to serve.

Nutritional Info: Calories: 131, Sodium: 67 mg, Dietary Fiber: 1.4 g, Fat: 6.4 g, Carbs: 14.7 g, Protein: 4 g.

Garlic Mashed Potatoes

Garlic Mashed Potatoes are a creamy, comforting side that will transform family dinner night or your next dinner party. Served best with roast duck, chicken or turkey this creamy side dish is to die for! Pair it with roasted vegetables and a glass of wine for something decadent and easy to whip up.

Servings: 6-8

Cook Time: 30 minutes

Ingredients

1-pound russet potatoes, peeled and cut into 2-inch chunks

2 garlic cloves, peeled and cut in half

1 cup sour cream

1 stick of butter, salted

1 tsp. sea salt

1 tsp. black pepper

1/2 cup milk

Instructions

1. Add 3 cups of water to the inner pot and place the potatoes and garlic in the steamer basket in the rice cooker. STEAM for 25 minutes, until very tender.

2. Meanwhile, combine the cream, 3/4 cup (1 1/2 sticks) of the butter; and the salt in a medium saucepan and heat until the cream simmers and the butter melts.

3. When the potatoes are tender, put them through a ricer or the medium blade of a food mill.

4. Transfer potatoes and garlic to a large mixing bowl. Add butter, sour cream, salt, pepper, and half the milk. Mash until butter starts to dissolve.

5. Add the other half of the milk and continue to mash until smooth.

6. If potatoes are still lumpy add an additional tablespoon of sour cream until they blend smooth.

7.   Return to the rice cooker inner pot and KEEP WARM until
     ready to serve.

Nutritional Info: Calories: 0, Sodium: 0 mg, Dietary Fiber: 0 g, Fat: 9.2 g, Carbs: 0 g,
Protein: 0 g.

Potato Salad

Potato Salad is one of the most versatile side dishes you can make. Great for parties, picnics, and tailgates — potato salad is also hearty and filling. Everyone will love this yummy, 'stick to your ribs' side dish.

Servings 4-6

Cook time 35 minutes

Ingredients

6 russet potatoes, peeled and cubed

1 1/2 cups water

3 eggs

1/4 cup sweet onion, chopped

1 cup red bell pepper, diced

1 cup sour cream

1/4 cup mayonnaise

1 tsp. yellow mustard

1/8 tsp. Worcestershire sauce

1/8 tsp. Sugar or sugar substitute

2 tbsp finely chopped celery

1 tbsp. dill pickle juice

Sea salt, for serving

Black pepper, for serving

Instructions

1. Add the water to the inner pot. Add potatoes and the eggs to the steamer basket. Lock the lid in place and set STEAM for 35 minutes; remove eggs at 25 minutes and place them in an ice bath to cool.

2. Return potatoes to STEAM for another 10 to 15 minutes or until tender, but not falling apart.

3. Combine onion, bell pepper, sour cream, mayo, yellow mustard, Worcestershire sauce, sugar, and pickle juice in a large mixing bowl.

4. Gently fold potatoes into the sour cream mixture.

5. Peel and chop the cooled eggs. Gently fold them into the potato salad.

6. Add sea salt and black pepper to taste.

7. Place in the refrigerator and chill at least one hour before serving.

Nutritional Info: Calories: 308, Sodium: 176 mg, Dietary Fiber: 5.6 g, Fat: 13.8 g, Carbs: 39.8 g, Protein: 8 g.

Sweet Potatoes

A savory, sweet side dish these Sweet Potatoes boast of a touch of South Africa. Garnish with butter, cinnamon, sea salt and black pepper to really bring out the rustic taste of this delicious side. Serve with your favorite meat or tofu for side dish fun.

Servings 4-6

Cook time 40 minutes

Ingredients

4 sweet potatoes, cut in half

2 cups water

Butter, for garnish

Cinnamon, for garnish

Sea salt, for garnish

Black pepper, for garnish

Instructions

1. Add 2 cups of water to the inner pot.
2. Add sweet potatoes to the steam basket, and place inside the rice cooker.
3. Lock lid in place and set to STEAM for 35 minutes.
4. Garnish with butter, cinnamon, sea salt and black pepper.

Nutritional Info: Calories: 44, Sodium: 61 mg, Dietary Fiber: 0.3 g, Fat: 1.6 g, Carbs: 7.4 g, Protein: 0.4 g.

Hummus

Hummus is a creamy treat that is out of this world! While you might traditionally serve it with pita bread, celery sticks and carrot sticks – this hummus is also delicious stuffed in chicken breasts for a quick and easy dinner. Another great way to enjoy this dish is to spread it on wraps and sandwiches for a healthy mayonnaise alternative.

Servings 2-4

Cook time 20 minutes

Ingredients

1 cup dry chickpeas, soaked

1 bay leaf

3 garlic cloves, crushed

3 tbsp. tahini

1 lemon, juiced

1/4 tsp. powdered cumin

1/2 tsp. sea salt

Paprika, to serve

Extra virgin olive oil, to serve

Instructions

1. Rinse the chickpeas and add to the inner pot of the rice cooker. Add two crushed garlic cloves and the Bay Leaf. Close and lock the lid and press RICE to 18 minutes.

2. Drain the chickpeas, reserving all of the cooking liquid. Discard the bay leaf and set aside to cool. Add chickpeas to a food processor or mash with a potato masher.

3. Fold one 1/2 cup of cooking liquid into the mash with the tahini, lemon juice, cumin and 1 fresh garlic clove (depending on your preference). Puree mix until creamy; if not at desired creaminess, fold in extra cooking liquid.

4. Dust with sea salt and paprika. Drizzle with olive oil. Enjoy alongside your favorite pita bread or veggie sticks.

Nutritional Info: Calories: 261, Sodium: 260 mg, Dietary Fiber: 10 g, Fat: 9.2 g, Carbs: 36 g, Protein: 11.9 g.

8

BREAKFAST RECIPES

Vanilla Yogurt Parfait

Yogurt is a delicious breakfast or even afternoon snack, and this recipe is so super easy. You'll be making tangy, sweet yogurt in the comfort of your own kitchen in no time with your MultiPot cooker.

Servings 1

Cook time 16 hours 15 minutes

Ingredients

4 1/4 cups milk

1/2 cup yogurt

1 tsp. pure vanilla extract

1 whole nectarine, sliced, for garnish

1/4 cup granola, for garnish

1 tsp. Honey, for garnish

Instructions

1. Add milk to inner pot of rice cooker and heat milk on YOGURT for 2 to 3 hours; until the candy thermometer reads 181 degrees Fahrenheit.

2. Fill a large container with ice and water. Place the inner pot of milk in to cool to 110 degrees Fahrenheit; be careful not to submerge it or get any water in the milk.

3. Remove one cup of the warm milk. Fold in the 1/2 cup of yogurt using a whisk. Next, whisk the mixture into the milk in the inner pot.

4. Place the inner pot of inoculated milk into the rice cooker, cover with a thick kitchen towel for 8 hours.

5. Fold in the vanilla extract gently until well-combined. Transfer the inner pot to the refrigerator to chill for 8 hours.

6. Once the yogurt is set, top yogurt with nectarines, honey, and granola to complete your breakfast parfait. Additionally, you can top yogurt with chocolate chunks, sliced bananas, and granola for a more decadent breakfast.

Nutritional Info: Calories: 503, Sodium: 667 mg, Dietary Fiber: 0 g, Fat: 4 g, Carbs: 63.9 g, Protein: 46 g.

Giant Rice Cooker Pancake with Maple Syrup and Berry Compote

If you love pancakes, you'll adore this mouthwatering recipe. Topped with sweet berry compote – you might even forego the syrup! Serve with coffee and orange juice for a truly decadent breakfast.

Servings 2-4

Cook time 50 minutes

Ingredients

2 cups unbleached, all-purpose flour

2 1/2 tsp. baking powder

2 tbsp. granulated white sugar or sugar substitute, plus 1 tsp. for Berry Compote

2 large eggs

1 1/2 cups low fat milk or almond milk

Butter, for serving

Maple syrup, for serving

1 cup of your favorite frozen berries, like strawberries and blueberries or mixed berries

Instructions:

1. Add eggs and milk to a large mixing bowl and whisk until completely blended. Fold in remaining ingredients and whisk until there are only a few small lumps remaining.

2. Grease the inner pot.

3. Pour the batter into the inner pot; be sure not to fill it too high as the pancake will get stuck to the lid.

4. Lock the rice cooker lid in place. Set to RICE for 45 minutes.

5. While pancake is cooking add berries, 1 tsp. sugar, and 1 cup water in a small saucepan. Cover and cook on medium heat for 10 minutes, shake the pan to stir but do not uncover the pot.

6. Insert a toothpick into the pancake, when it removes cleanly the pancake is done. Remove the pancake by flipping the inner pot upside down over a large plate.

7. Remove Berry Compote from stove top and stir with a spoon to make sure it's at the desired thickness.

8. Top pancake with butter, syrup and berry compote. As a Gluten Free Alternative: Use your favorite gluten-free flour or recipe and enjoy!

Nutritional Info: Calories: 332, Sodium: 79 mg, Dietary Fiber: 3 g, Fat: 4.1 g, Carbs: 60.2 g, Protein: 12.9 g.

Sausage and Grits Breakfast Casserole

Sausage and grits is a southern tradition when it comes to a hearty breakfast. This delicious recipe will have you whipping up something hearty in no time! A one dish treat that's sure to please the whole family.

Servings 6

Cook time 1 hour 10 minutes

Ingredients

2 cups water

1/2 cup quick grits

1/2 tsp. sea salt

1 tbsp. butter

1/2 tsp. black pepper

1/8 tsp. garlic powder

1/2 lb. breakfast sausage, cooked and crumbled

1 cup white cheddar cheese, shredded

2 eggs

1/4 cup milk

Instructions

1. Add the water, grits, and salt to the inner pot of the rice cooker and stir to combine.

2. Lock the lid in place and cook on RICE for 30 minutes.

3. Add eggs and milk to a small mixing bowl. Beat with a whisk until well combined and set aside away from direct heat.

4. Turn the rice cooker OFF.

5. Open the lid and stir the grits; get the bottom with a spatula to ensure grits aren't stuck.

6. Stir in the butter until melted.

7. Fold in the remaining spices, cooked sausage, and cheese.

8. Fold the egg mixture into the grit mix turning over again and lock the lid into place.

9. Press FLASH RICE and cook for 15 minutes; when the setting turns to warm turn the rice cooker OFF, open the lid, and stir.

10. Lock lid back into place and set to FLASH RICE for 15 additional minutes.

11. Serve immediately with your favorite breakfast beverage when the second cooking cycle is done.

Nutritional Info: Calories: 259, Sodium: 598 mg, Dietary Fiber: 0.1 g, Fat: 20.6 g, Carbs: 3.4 g, Protein: 14.5 g.

Hard Boiled Eggs

Hard-boiled eggs are heart healthy and delicious. High in protein, they are a great way to start the day. Serve with whole grain toast and avocado for a more filling breakfast option.

Servings 1

Cook Time 18 minutes

Ingredients

2 eggs   2 cups water

Instructions

1.   Pour the water into the inner pot.

2.   Add 2 eggs to steamer basket and place in the rice cooker.

3.   Lock lid in place. Press EGG and cook for 15 minutes.

4.   Transfer eggs to an ice bath of cold water for 1 to 3 minutes. Peel, and enjoy!

5.   Note: you can cook 1 to 12 eggs in the MultiPot, so the recipe can be changed depending on how many eggs you need.

Nutritional Info: Calories: 126, Sodium: 137 mg, Dietary Fiber: 0 g, Fat: 8.8 g, Carbs: 0.7 g, Protein: 11.1 g.

Whole Grain Porridge

Whole grain porridge is a very healthy breakfast option for those who are looking out for their heart. But when it comes to eating low cholesterol this whole grain porridge is just the treat for you. You can whip it up in no time, and feel full all morning long.

Servings 4

Cook Time 55 minutes

Ingredients

- 1/2 cup wild rice
- 1/2 cup steel-cut oats
- 1/2 cup wheat cereal
- 1 (2-inch) slice of an orange peel
- 1 cinnamon stick
- 2 tsp. light brown sugar or brown sugar substitute
- 1/4 teaspoon sea salt
- 1/4 cup dried cranberries, cherries, raisins or chopped apricots
- Chopped nuts, serving
- Honey, for serving
- Milk or milk substitute like Coconut milk, for serving

Instructions

1. Add rice, oats, and wheat cereal to the inner pot.

2. Stir in the orange peel, cinnamon stick, sugar, sea salt, dried fruit, and 5 cups of filtered water.

3. Lock the lid and program the DELAY TIMER on MULTIGRAIN for 12 hours; remember this has a 50-minute cooking time, so include that in the calculation of what time you want to serve breakfast.

4. Add milk if desired and serve the whole grain porridge warm topped with nuts and honey.

Nutritional Info: Calories: 128, Sodium: 121 mg, Dietary Fiber: 3.3 g, Fat: 0.7 g, Carbs: 27 g, Protein: 4.5 g.

Huevos Rancheros

A traditional Mexican Cuisine, this Huevos Rancheros recipe is the perfect breakfast for those who love q little spice in their life. Easy to whip up in no time with the MultiPot, this recipe will become a family favorite in no time.

Servings 6-8

Cook time 40 minutes

Ingredients

1 tbsp. butter

10 eggs, beaten

1 cup light whipping cream

1 1/2 cups Mexican blend cheese, shredded

1/2 tsp. pepper

1/2 tsp. chili powder

1/2 tsp. garlic powder

1/2 tsp. cumin powder

Pinch of nutmeg

1 (4 oz.) can green chilies, drained

1 (10 oz.) can red enchilada sauce

1/2 cup cheddar cheese, shredded

8 tortillas, warmed

Instructions

1. Grease the inner pot with the butter.

2. Combine eggs, cream, mexican cheese, and spices in a large mixing bowl.

3. Fold in the chilies and pour into the inner pot.

4. Lock lid into place and cook on RICE for 30 minutes.

5. Remove lid and top with enchilada sauce and cheddar cheese. Replace lid and cook an additional 15 minutes or until cheese is melted.

6. Top tortillas with huevos and serve immediately with your favorite breakfast drink!

Nutritional Info: Calories: 327, Sodium: 719 mg, Dietary Fiber: 1.9 g, Fat: 22.6 g, Carbs: 15.8 g, Protein: 15.9 g.

Old Fashioned Oatmeal

Old Fashioned Oatmeal is a great breakfast treat that will surely fill you up to get your day started. No matter how you like your oats, this recipe will transform your taste buds at breakfast. Creamy oats have never been so easy when you whip them up in your MultiPot.

Servings 1

Cook time 21 minutes

Ingredients

1/2 cup rolled oats

1 cup water

1 pinch of sea salt

Milk or almond milk, for serving

Honey, for serving

Cinnamon, for serving

Instructions

1. Add all of the ingredients to the inner pot of the rice cooker.

2. Press the RICE button and allow to cook until timer beeps.

3. Open the lid and stir the oats.

4. Fold in milk, honey, and cinnamon, if desired, and serve while hot.

Nutritional Info: Calories: 155, Sodium: 244 mg, Dietary Fiber: 4.1 g, Fat: 2.7 g, Carbs: 27.7 g, Protein: 5.4 g.

Slow-Cooked Blueberry French Toast

If you are a connoisseur of French toast, this recipe is for you. Slow cooked to Perfection with blueberries right in the middle you will love this deliciously decadent French toast. Serve it with a glass of champagne or sparkling water for one scrumptious brunch.

Servings 12

Cook time 1 hour

INGREDIENTS

Non-stick cooking spray

8 large eggs

1/2 cup plain yogurt

1/3 cup sour cream

1 tsp. vanilla extract

1/2 tsp. ground cinnamon

1 cup milk or milk substitute

1/3 cup maple syrup

1 loaf of French or Italian bread, cubed

1 1/2 cups fresh or frozen blueberries

12 ounces cream cheese, cubed

Maple syrup, for serving

Instructions

1. Add eggs, yogurt, sour cream, vanilla, and cinnamon to a large mixing bowl; stir to combine. Gradually whisk in milk and maple syrup until blended.

2. Grease the inner pot of the rice cooker with cooking spray. Add half the cubed bread to inner pot; layer with half of the blueberries, cream cheese, and egg mixture. Add a second layer of bread cubes, then the other half of the blueberries, cream cheese, and egg mixture.

3. Cover and refrigerate overnight.

4. Remove French Toast from the refrigerator 30 minutes before cooking. Place inner pot in the rice cooker. Lock lid and set to STEAM for 1 hour or until a knife inserted in the center comes out clean.

5.   Serve with maple syrup and enjoy!

Nutritional Info: Calories: 266, Sodium: 185 mg, Dietary Fiber: 0.6 g, Fat: 15.2 g, Carbs: 14.4 g, Protein: 8.4 g.

Western Omelette Quiche

If you love the taste of a western omelet you are going to adore this quiche recipe. Easy to make, in just under an hour, you'll have everyone fall in love with the MultiPot Pressure Cooker with this breakfast dish.

Servings 4-6

Cook time 40 minutes

Ingredients

6 large eggs, well beaten

1/3 cup half and half

1/8 tsp. sea salt

1/8 tsp. ground black pepper

1/8 tsp. chili powder

1/8 tsp. garlic powder

1/2 cup ham, diced

1/2 cup bell peppers, diced

1/4 cup sweet onion, diced

3/4 cups cheddar cheese, shredded

Instructions

1. Add 1 1/2 cups of water to the inner pot. Butter or spray an 8-inch souffle dish and set aside. Whisk together the eggs, half and half, and spices in a large mixing bowl.

2. Add diced ham, peppers, onions, and cheese to the soufflé dish and stir to mix well. Pour egg mixture over the top of the veggies and ham and stir to combine.

3. Cover the souffle dish with a silicone lid or aluminum foil loosely. Use the aluminum foil to create a sling and lower the souffle dish into the inner pot of the rice cooker.

4. Lock the rice cooker lid in place and press EGG button for 30 minutes. Open the lid, lift out the souffle dish and remove the foil carefully.

5. Serve immediately with an iced tea or cup of coffee!

Nutritional Info: Calories: 170, Sodium: 350 mg, Dietary Fiber: 0.4 g, Fat: 12.2 g, Carbs: 2.9 g, Protein: 12.3 g.

Rice Cooker Summer Vegetable Frittata

Summer vegetable frittatas are absolutely delicious when it comes to cooking a healthy breakfast for you and your family. While we've suggested some delicious vegetables below, you can use just about any vegetable you really love in this mouth-watering recipe. Just follow the same directions and you've got one savory breakfast treat.

Servings 2-4

Cook time

Ingredients

6 large eggs

1 tsp. milk

2 tbsp. parmesan cheese shaved

2 tsp. olive oil

1/3 cup sweet onion, diced

1 small carrot, diced

1 small red bell pepper, diced

1 small zucchini, diced

1/8 tsp. garlic powder

1/8 tsp. sea salt

1/8 tsp. black pepper

Instructions

1. Heat a frying pan to medium and add 1 tsp. olive oil. Add vegetables, season with salt, pepper, and garlic. Cook for 10 minutes.

2. Whisk eggs and milk in a mixing bowl until yolks are well incorporated with egg whites. Fold in parmesan.

3. Add egg mixture to the greased inner pot. Add the vegetables and distribute them evenly in the egg mixture with a spatula.

4. Press RICE. Serve immediately with your favorite juice, sparkling water or hot beverage.

Nutritional Info: Calories: 174, Sodium: 242 mg, Dietary Fiber: 1.3 g, Fat: 11.5 g, Carbs: 6.4 g, Protein: 12.6 g.

9

LUNCH RECIPES

Buddha Bowl

The latest lunch sensation with clean eating in mind this recipe can be made right in your rice cooker for a quick, easy lunch. The Buddha Bowl is inspired by the latest wave of Clean Eating, Paleo, vegan, and vegetarian lunch options. Don't forget to enjoy this one with a glass of your favorite sparkling water.

Servings 2-4

Cook time 40 minutes

Ingredients

4 tablespoons extra-virgin olive oil, divided

1 large sweet potato, peeled and cut into 11/2-inch pieces

1 cup quinoa, rinsed and drained

1 large clove garlic, minced

1/2 teaspoon sea salt

2 small carrots, peeled and cut in half

1 stalk Chinese broccoli

4 cups chopped kale

2 cups water

1 tablespoon lime juice

1 (15 oz.) can chickpeas, drained and rinsed for garnish

unsalted pistachios, for garnish

1 whole avocado, sliced for garnish

Instructions

1. Heat 2 tablespoons of olive oil over medium heat in a large frying pan. Add sweet potato, broccoli, carrots, quinoa, garlic and sea salt. Cook, while stirring, until the garlic is fragrant; about 3 minutes.

2. Add the quinoa mixture to the inner pot of the rice cooker. Stir in kale and water.

3. Lock the lid in place and press RICE for 20 minutes.

4. Remove the lid and let stand for 5 minutes.

5.   Combine the remaining 2 tablespoons of olive oil, and lime juice in a small mixing bowl. Divide the quinoa mixture among 2 to 4 bowls.

6.   Top each portion with chickpeas, pistachios and sliced avocado. Drizzle with the lime dressing and serve!

Nutritional Info: Calories: 775, Sodium: 332 mg, Dietary Fiber: 25.4 g, Fat: 25.1 g, Carbs: 113 g, Protein: 30.5 g.

Chipotle Chicken Bowls with Cilantro Lime Rice

If you're looking to spice up your lunch hour, this Chipotle chicken bowl with cilantro lime rice will do just the trick. A taste of the Southwest mixed with the influence of the Middle East, this delicious and healthy lunch option will have you packing more lunch for work or school.

Servings 4

Cook time 50 minutes

Ingredients

1 cup quinoa, rinsed and drained

1 cup water

1/8 tsp. kosher salt

1/2 tsp. ground cumin

pinch black pepper

1 tablespoon chipotle paste

1 cup medium salsa

1 lb. boneless, skinless chicken thighs

1 (15 oz.) black beans

1/4 tsp. sea salt

1 lime, juiced

2 tsp. olive oil

2 tbsp. chopped cilantro

1 cup halved cherry tomatoes, for serving

1 avocado, sliced, for serving

4 lime wedges, for garnish

Instructions

1. Add quinoa and water to the inner pot. Cook on RICE for 18 to 22 minutes, or until all the liquid is absorbed. Fluff with a fork. Stir in the lime juice, olive oil, and cilantro; set aside.

2. Combine the salt, cumin black pepper, chipotle, and salsa in a medium mixing bowl.

3. Add the chicken to the inner pot of the rice cooker and pour the salsa mixture over the chicken. Cook on POULTRY for 20 minutes.

4. Add the black beans and cook an additional 2 minutes.

5. Transfer chicken and beans to a bowl.

6.   Equally distribute quinoa, chicken, and beans to each bowl. Top with cherry tomatoes and sliced avocado. Serve with lime wedges and enjoy.

Nutritional Info: Calories: 696, Sodium: 414 mg, Dietary Fiber: 18.4 g, Fat: 25.4 g, Carbs: 68 g, Protein: 52 g.

Lemon Chicken with Zucchini Noodles

If you're counting ketos, this recipe is absolutely delicious and right up your alley. Lemon chicken with zucchini noodles is a delicious no carb option for those looking to go gluten-free. Prep it on the weekend and pack it for lunch all week and you've got a perfectly healthy option.

Servings 3

Cook Time 20 minutes

Ingredients

8 boneless chicken thighs

1 tbsp. smoked paprika

1 tbsp. unsalted butter, divided

1 tsp. olive oil

3 cloves garlic, minced

1 cup chicken broth

1/4 cup Parmesan shaved

1 lemon, juiced

1 teaspoon dried thyme

1/2 cup baby spinach, chopped

2 cups zucchini noodles

Sea salt and freshly ground black pepper, to taste

Instructions

1. Add all ingredients to the inner pot and stir.

2. Place inner pot in the rice cooker, close lid, and press RICE. Allow cooking until rice cooker switches to KEEP WARM

3. Remove and transfer to plates. Season with sea salt and black pepper. Serve immediately as a main course.

Nutritional Info: Calories: 428, Sodium: 433 mg, Dietary Fiber: 3.6 g, Fat: 29.5 g, Carbs: 10.4 g, Protein: 30.7 g.

BBQ Pork Chops with Steamed Apples

Barbecue pork chops with steamed apples are easy and delicious. raising them for hours in order to have succulent ribs. You can do it right in your rice cooker, and serve it on a bed of greens for a healthy lunch.

Servings 4

Cook time 45 minutes

Ingredients

4 bone-in pork chops

2 tbsp. olive oil

BBQ Seasoning

BBQ sauce

1 1/2 cups chicken broth

1 apple, sliced

Instructions

1. Rub both sides of each pork chop with your favorite BBQ seasoning.

2. Press RICE and add olive oil to the inner pot. Brown each pork chop on both sides, one at a time, and transfer to a plate.

3. Add in chicken broth to inner pot; use a spatula to scrape the browned bits off the bottom of the pan.

4. Add pork chops to the inner pot with 1/3 cup of BBQ Sauce; reserve the rest for serving.

5. Add apple slices to the steam basket. Press STEAM and cook 30 minutes.

6. Remove apples and transfer to a plate. Transfer pork chops to a baking sheet. Baste with remaining BBQ sauce and place under an oven broiler, on high, for 2-3 minutes to caramelize. Serve immediately.

Nutritional Info: Calories: 151, Sodium: 394 mg, Dietary Fiber: 1.4 g, Fat: 10.3 g, Carbs: 8.3 g, Protein: 7.3 g.

Orange Chicken

If you love the taste of restaurant-inspired orange chicken, you are going to love this recipe. This orange chicken is succulent and delicious served on a bed of rice or with your favorite vegetables. Quick and easy you'll have lunch made in no time every day of the week.

Servings 6

Cook time 30 minutes

Ingredients

2 lbs. chicken thighs, cut into 1-2-inch pieces

2 tbsp. grapeseed oil

1 cup no sugar added orange juice, plus 2 tbsp.

1 tbsp. ginger, grated

3 cloves garlic, minced

1 tbsp. mirin

1/3 cup brown sugar or sugar substitute

1/4 cup soy sauce

1 tsp. red chili pepper

zest from 1 orange

2 tablespoons cornstarch

2 tablespoons orange juice

Instructions

1. Add the grapeseed oil and press MULTIGRAIN. Add chicken and sauté for 2-3 minutes, stirring constantly; cook until it just starts to get golden.

2. Transfer chicken to a plate and deglaze the pot with 1/4 cup orange juice and scrape chicken bits off with a spatula.

3. Add the remaining 3/4 cups of orange juice, minced garlic, ginger, soy sauce, brown sugar, mirin, orange zest and red chili flakes to the inner pot.

4. Stir gently until all the ingredients are combined and fold in the chicken.

5. Close lid and press POULTRY for 15 minutes.

6. Combine 2 tbsp. cornstarch with 2 tbsp. orange juice in a small mixing bowl: whisk until there are no lumps.

7. Gently fold the cornstarch mixture into the inner pot. STEAM an additional 3 minutes.

8. Uncover and let the Orange Chicken stand for 5 minutes and serve over rice.

Nutritional Info: Calories: 405, Sodium: 754 mg, Dietary Fiber: 0.4 g, Fat: 15.9 g, Carbs: 18.4 g, Protein: 44.9 g.

Garlic Drumsticks

Garlic drumsticks are a healthy way to enjoy chicken without the saturated fat. You can whip up healthy chicken drumsticks in less than 30 minutes for lunch with this delicious recipe.

Servings 4-6

Cook time 24 minutes

Ingredients

8 chicken drumsticks

1/4 cup water

1 tsp. sesame oil

1/2 cup dark soy sauce

2 tbsp. honey

2 tbsp. mirin

2 garlic cloves, minced

1 tsp. fresh ginger, minced

1/2 sweet onion, chopped

Instructions

1. Add all of the ingredients to the inner pot of the rice cooker. Press POULTRY for 30 minutes.

2. Let chicken rest on WARM for 5 minutes before opening the pot.

3. Transfer the drumsticks a cookie sheet lined with parchment paper. Broil the chicken on high for 2 minutes on each side.

4. Transfer chicken to a platter and serve with leftover sauce in the rice cooker.

Nutritional Info: Calories: 155, Sodium: 602 mg, Dietary Fiber: 0.3 g, Fat: 4.3 g, Carbs: 11.6 g, Protein: 17.2 g.

Steamed Dumplings with Asian Salad

One of the most delicious and healthy dishes you can make for lunch is steamed dumplings with Asian salad. This traditionally inspired dish is something that is both healthy and delicious to eat.

Servings 2

Cook Time 20 minutes

Ingredients

12 frozen dumplings

2 cups water

Sesame oil, for cooking and serving

Soy sauce, for serving

Instructions

1. Add water to the inner pot of the rice cooker.

2. Use a paper towel to apply a light coat of sesame oil to the surface of the steam basket.

3. Arrange the dumplings in a single layer in the steam basket and place the basket in the bowl of the rice cooker.

4. Lock the lid in place and press STEAM for 20 minutes.

5. Open the rice cooker and let the dumplings rest for 5 minutes to allow the excess moisture on the surface of the dumplings to evaporate.

6. Remove the steaming basket from the rice cooker and transfer the steamed dumplings to a serving tray. Serve with sesame oil and soy sauce for dipping and enjoy!

Nutritional Info: Calories: 510, Sodium: 387 mg, Dietary Fiber: 3 g, Fat: 7.5 g, Carbs: 69 g, Protein: 39 g.

Mongolian Beef

If you really want lunch catered it in, you can whip up this Mongolian beef right in the comfort of your kitchen without even visiting the restaurant. You'll serve lunch in less than 30 minutes with this amazing recipe.

Servings 4

Cook time 20 minutes

Ingredients

1 1/2 lbs. Flank steak

3/4 cups soy sauce

1 tsp. garlic powder

1/8 tsp. white pepper

1/2 cup brown sugar or brown sugar substitute

1/4 cup water

1/2 teaspoon fresh ginger, minced

1 carrot, shredded

1 tablespoon grapeseed oil

3 tbsp. cornstarch

3 tbsp. Water

1 green onion sliced, for garnish

Instructions

1. Add the grapeseed oil and press MULTIGRAIN. Add the beef and sauté for 2 minutes, stirring constantly; cook until it just starts to brown.

2. Add the soy sauce, garlic powder, white pepper, brown sugar, water, ginger and carrot to inner pot.

3. Stir gently until all the ingredients are combined.

4. Close lid and press MEAT for 15 minutes.

5. Combine 2 tbsp. cornstarch with 2 tbsp. water in a small mixing bowl: whisk until there are no lumps.

6. Gently fold the cornstarch mixture into the inner pot. STEAM an additional 3 minutes.

7. Uncover and let the Mongolian Beef stand for 5 minutes and serve over rice, garnished with green onions.

Nutritional Info: Calories: 487, Sodium: 287 mg, Dietary Fiber: 1 g, Fat: 17.6 g, Carbs: 29.2 g, Protein: 50.7 g.

Beef Gyros

Serve a taste of Greece for lunch with these delicious beef Gyros. Healthy and delicious, if you're following the Mediterranean diet this is the perfect lunch for you.

Servings 4

Cook time 20 minutes

Ingredients

1 lb. beef tenderloin, thinly sliced

1 tsp. dried parsley

1 tsp, black pepper

1 tsp. sea salt

1/2 tsp. oregano

1/2 tsp. basil

1/3 cup red onion, thinly sliced

2 cloves garlic, minced

1/2 cup beef or vegetable broth

1 tbsp lemon juice

Balsamic vinegar, for garnish

1 tsp. olive oil, plus more for garnish

4 whole wheat pitas, cut in half

Sliced tomatoes, for garnish

Sliced onions, for garnish

Sliced cucumbers, for garnish

Lettuce, for garnish

Fresh buffalo mozzarella, thin sliced, optional garnish

Instructions

1. Add 1 tsp. Olive oil to inner pot and heat on RICE for 2 minutes.

2. Add meat, seasoning, and red onion, and garlic to inner pot. Cook for 5 minutes.

3. Pour lemon juice and broth over the meat, stir, and lock lid into place.

4. Press STEAM for 10 minutes.

5. Transfer meat to a plate; discard broth and red onion.

6.   To assemble Gyros, stuff each pita half with a few slices of meat, lettuce, tomato, cucumber, onions, and mozzarella.

7.   Drizzle with vinegar and olive oil and serve.

Nutritional Info: Calories: 431, Sodium: 974 mg, Dietary Fiber: 5.2 g, Fat: 17.6 g, Carbs: 29.2 g, Protein: 50.7 g.

Tavern Burgers

When you really want a burger for lunch, this recipe will get it done in no time. No more waiting in line at a drive-thru, you can get a tasty tavern-style burgers right in the comfort of your own kitchen within 20 minutes.

Servings 6-8

Cook time 20 minutes

Ingredients

2 lbs. lean ground beef

1 tsp. onion, finely chopped

1/2 tsp. sea salt

1/4 tsp. black pepper

1 tsp. Cajun seasoning

1 (10.75 oz) can tomato soup

Yellow mustard, for serving

Swiss cheese slices, for serving

Lettuce, for serving

Sandwich Buns, split, for serving

Instructions

1. Add ground beef, onion, sea salt, black pepper, cajun seasoning and tomato soup to the inner pot. Cook on STEAM for 30 minutes; let rest on KEEP WARM for five minutes.

2. Assemble sandwiches by spooning beef onto bottom slice of bun. Top with favorite toppings and serve hot!

Nutritional Info: Calories: 234, Sodium: 408 mg, Dietary Fiber: 0.5 g, Fat: 7.3 g, Carbs: 5.2 g, Protein: 35 g.

Jacket Potatoes

Simple and easy jacket potatoes are a quick lunch option. When it comes to staying healthy without the high-fiber carbs, whip up these jacket potatoes and top it with your favorite toppings.

Servings 4

Cook time 21 minutes

Ingredients

4 medium baking potatoes

Butter, for serving

Sea salt, for serving

Black pepper, for serving

Sour cream, for serving

Instructions

1. Fill the inner pot with 1 cup of water.
2. Prick the potatoes, all over, with a fork. Place them in the steamer basket.
3. Lock the lid in place and set to STEAM for 20 minutes.
4. Serve with sea salt, black pepper, butter and sour cream.

Nutritional Info: Calories: 129, Sodium: 17 mg, Dietary Fiber: 2.3 g, Fat: 0.2 g, Carbs: 30.4 g, Protein: 3.5 g.

Egg Mayo Sandwiches

Egg Mayo sandwiches are a delicious light lunch that can be cooked in no time. When you fire up the MultiPot Pressure Cooker you can make delicious egg Mayo sandwiches in less than no time. Pack them up and take them on the go or enjoy them right at home.

Servings 2

Cook Time 30 minutes

Ingredients

5 eggs	1/8 tsp. Sea salt
2 cups water	1/8 tsp. Black pepper
6 tbsp. mayonnaise	Pinch of nutmeg
1/3 cup parmesan cheese shaved	Pinch of brown sugar or sugar substitute
1 tsp. mustard powder	Four slices of your favorite bread or 2 baguettes
1 tsp. parsley	

Instructions

1. Pour water into the inner pot.

2. Add 5 eggs to steamer basket and place in the rice cooker.

3. Lock lid in place. Press EGG and cook for 15 minutes.

4. Transfer eggs to an ice bath of cold water for 3 to 5 minutes.

5. Peel, and add to a large mixing bowl. Mash with a fork, and fold in remaining ingredients. Stir to combine well.

6. Top bread or stuff baguette with egg mayo; any remaining egg may be refrigerated for later use.

Nutritional Info: Calories: 356, Sodium: 660 mg, Dietary Fiber: 0.3 g, Fat: 27.5 g, Carbs: 12.1 g, Protein: 16.2 g.

Pulled Chicken Tacos

Pulled chicken tacos are a delicious Cantina treat right in the comfort of your kitchen. A delicious healthy alternative to fried tacos, these pulled chicken tacos are packed with antioxidants and the right amount of spice.

Servings 4-6

Cook time 35 minutes

Ingredients

4 boneless, skinless chicken thighs

1 tbsp. chili powder

1 tbsp. ground cumin

1 tsp. smoked paprika

1 tsp. dried oregano

1 tsp. garlic powder

1 tsp. sea salt

2 limes, juiced

1 cup chicken broth

6 corn tortillas

Lettuce, shredded for serving

Guacamole, for serving

Sour cream, for serving

Hot sauce, for serving

Cotija cheese, for serving

Instructions

1. Add chicken, spices, chicken broth and lime juice to the inner pot.

2. Cook on POULTRY for 25 minutes.

3. Remove chicken and pull using a fork to shred. Transfer chicken back to pot and cook for additional 5 to 10 minutes.

4. Remove chicken and discard broth.

5. Top tortillas with guacamole, chicken, lettuce, sour cream, cheese and hot sauce to serve.

Nutritional Info: Calories: 160, Sodium: 532 mg, Dietary Fiber: 2.4 g, Fat: 4.4 g, Carbs: 13.9 g, Protein: 17.4 g.

Beefy Broccoli Noodles and Cheese

This recipe is specifically for those who love leftovers! Many people wonder what to do with a leftover Sunday Roast, and we've got the perfect idea for you. Think ooey, gooey beefy noodles that are the perfect comfort food to transform leftover dinners.

Servings 4

Cook time 30 minutes

Ingredients

2 cups leftover beef roast, like London Broil

2 cups egg noodles

2 cups beef broth

1/2 tsp. sea salt

2 cups broccoli florets, chopped

1 cup milk or milk substitute like Almond

1 1/2 cups mozzarella cheese, shredded

Instructions

1. Combine the beef, broth, noodles, broccoli, and salt in the rice cooker. Lock lid in place and cook on RICE for 15 minutes.

2. Open the lid and fold in the milk and cheese.

3. Lock the lid and STEAM and additional 10 minutes; when ready the cheese will be melted, and the milk well-incorporated.

4. Serve immediately and enjoy.

Nutritional Info: Calories: 285, Sodium: 742 mg, Dietary Fiber: 2.1 g, Fat: 8.9 g, Carbs: 27 g, Protein: 24 g.

Rice Cooker Braised Chicken Wings

If you love chicken wings, but don't like them deep-fried this recipe is for you. These delicious rice cooker braised chicken wings will really hit the spot when it comes to indulging for lunch.

Servings 1-2

Cook time 35 minutes

Ingredients

12 chicken wings

1 tsp. honey

2 tbsp. sesame oil

1 tsp. rice wine

1 tbsp. fresh ginger, sliced

1/8 tsp. white pepper

2 tsp. dark soy sauce

1/2 tsp. sea salt

Instructions

1. Rinse the chicken wings thoroughly in cold water. Dry them with a paper towel.

2. Add remaining ingredients to a large mixing bowl and stir to combine well. Add chicken wings and toss to coat.

3. Add the chicken wings to the inner pot reserving half the sauce for later. Press POULTRY and cook 30 minutes.

4. Flip the wings after 30 minutes, add remaining sauce and cook an additional 45 minutes.

5. Serve with extra sauce or soy sauce as desired!

Nutritional Info: Calories: 531, Sodium: 852 mg, Dietary Fiber: 0.7 g, Fat: 39.1 g, Carbs: 19.7 g, Protein: 25.3 g.

Mango Cucumber Rice Salad

Why salad is absolutely delicious and super healthy for those who are watching their weight. This Fresh Salad is a great take on all things rice cooker. For a super healthy delicious lunch, you will love this recipe.

Servings 6

Cook time 35 minutes

Ingredients

1 1/2 cups rice

1/2 cup quinoa, rinsed

2 cups water

Juice of 1 lime, plus 1 tsp. zest

2 tbsp. olive oil

1 tsp. sugar

1 tsp. coarse ground pepper

1 tsp. garlic powder

1 cup mango, diced

1 cucumber, peeled, seeded and diced

1 jalapeno, seeded and thinly sliced

1/3 cup chopped fresh cilantro

Instructions

1. Add rice, quinoa, and water to the inner pot. Press RICE and cook for 30 minutes.

2. Combine lime, zest, olive oil, sugar and spices in a large mixing bowl. Fold in mango, cucumber, jalapeno, and cilantro.

3. Fluff rice mixture with a fork and evenly distribute to bowls. Top with a large scoop of mango mixture and serve.

Nutritional Info: Calories: 292, Sodium: 7 mg, Dietary Fiber: 2.5 g, Fat: 6 g, Carbs: 53.8 g, Protein: 6 g.

10

SOUPS, CHILI, STEWS, SOUFFLES

Rice Cooker Chili

When you were looking for something warm and Hearty on a cold day, this rice cooker chili hits the spot. Hearty and delicious you can serve this soup up alone or with oyster crackers and a lager.

Servings 6-8

Cook time

Ingredients

1 lb. ground beef

1 (15 oz.) can chopped tomatoes, no-sodium added

1 (15 oz.) can pinto beans

1 (15 oz.) can red kidney beans, in chili sauce

1 tbsp. chili powder

1 cup tomato sauce

1/8 tsp. sugar

2 tsp. dried oregano

1 green bell pepper, diced

1 small onion, diced

Salt and pepper to taste

Instructions

1. Add ground beef into the rice cooker and cook on SAUTE until browned; drain the excess fat.

2. Add remaining ingredients and SOUP for 30 minutes to 1 hour.

3. Enjoy topped with cheese, sour cream, or additional diced onions. Alternatively, you can omit the beef for vegetarians and add lentils or swap the beef for turkey for a healthy choice.

Nutritional Info: Calories: 498, Sodium: 223 mg, Dietary Fiber: 18.3 g, Fat: 5.2 g, Carbs: 72.3 g, Protein: 41.9 g.

Taco Soup

If you are looking to try something different with your MultiPot Pressure Cooker this taco soup recipe is just what you've been looking for. With the right amount of spice and secret ingredients, you'll have your family wanting taco soup every day of the week.

Servings 6

Cook time 1 hour

Ingredients

1 lb. chicken breast or tenders, diced

1 (15 oz) can hominy

1/2 medium onion, diced

1 clove garlic, minced

2 tsp. olive oil

5 cups chicken broth, low-sodium

1 (15 oz.) can diced tomatoes

1/2 cup brown rice

1/2 cup black beans, canned

Tortilla chips, for serving

Shredded cheese, for serving

Instructions

1. Add olive oil to inner pot and heat for 2 minutes on SAUTE; add onion and garlic and saute for 2 minutes.

2. Add diced chicken and brown for about 5 to 10 minutes.

3. Add remaining ingredients to the inner pot and cook on SOUP for 45 minutes to 1 hour and serve topped with tortilla chips and shredded cheese.

Nutritional Info: Calories: 312, Sodium: 829 mg, Dietary Fiber: 5.8 g, Fat: 6 g, Carbs: 36.8 g, Protein: 26.6 g.

White Chicken Chili

For those who want a lighter alternative to a hearty beef chili, this white chicken chili hits the spot. White chicken chili is delicious for tailgates and football parties and is a fan-favorite loved by everyone.

Servings 6

Cook time 25 minutes

Ingredients

1 lb. skinless boneless chicken thighs

5 cups chicken broth

2 garlic cloves, minced

1 medium onion, diced

1 (4.5 oz.) can green chilies

2 (15 oz.) cans can white northern beans, do not drain

1/2 tsp. dried oregano

1 tsp. ground cumin

1 tsp. chili powder

1 tsp. sea salt

1 tsp. ground black pepper

Instructions

1. Add all of the ingredients to the inner pot.

2. Cook on SOUP for 25 minutes.

3. Carefully remove the chicken thighs and use a fork and knife to shred the chicken.

4. Return chicken to the inner pot and STEAM an additional 5 minutes.

5. Serve hot!

Nutritional Info: Calories: 285, Sodium: 1172 mg, Dietary Fiber: 4.3 g, Fat: 7.3 g, Carbs: 15.9 g, Protein: 37.8 g

Chicken Daikon Soup

When you're feeling under the weather try this chicken daikon soup as a homemade alternative. You can whip this up in no time, and have a delicious soup that you can freeze and reheat for weeks to come.

Serves 2-3

Cook Time 3 hrs.

Ingredients

1 lb. boneless, skinless chicken thighs

1 tsp. ginger, freshly sliced

1 daikon, peeled and cut into large chunks

1 small carrot, peeled and shredded

8 shiitake mushrooms, sliced and stems removed

1 tbsp. goji berries

3 conpoy or dried scallops

1/8 tsp. sea salt

Instructions

1. Add 4 cups of water to the inner pot and STEAM for 10 minutes; discard liquid and set aside blanched chicken pieces.

2. Add another 4 cups of water to the rice cooker pot. Add chicken and remaining ingredients.

3. Lock the lid in place and press SOUP for 45 minutes; allow to simmer for 1 hour on KEEP WARM when the SOUP cycle is done.

4. Enjoy hot!

Nutritional Info: Calories: 344, Sodium: 738 mg, Dietary Fiber: 5.7 g, Fat: 7.1 g, Carbs: 36.2 g, Protein: 38 g

Hearty Red Wine Stew

For those lazy Sundays when you want to meal prep in the winter, this hearty red wine stew is just for you. Filled with chunks of beef and red potatoes, this delicious healthy alternative is really great for those who are looking out for their heart.

Servings 6-8

Cook time 2 hours

Ingredients

2 pounds beef chuck, cut into 1 1/2 inch cubes

2 tbsp. all-purpose flour

1 tsp. garlic powder

1 tsp. sea salt

1 tsp. black pepper

1 tbsp. olive oil

3 shallots, peeled and quartered

1 lb. small red potatoes halved

3 medium carrots, sliced large

3 sprigs fresh thyme

2 sprigs fresh rosemary

1 (15 oz.) can petite diced tomatoes

1 tbsp. balsamic vinegar

1 cup red wine

2 cups low-sodium beef broth

Instructions

1. Toss the beef cubes with the flour, garlic powder, salt and pepper to coat.

2. Add all the ingredients and toss well to combine.

3. Set to MEAT/STEW for 2 hours.

4. Ladle the stew into bowls and serve with your favorite, fresh bread.

Nutritional Info: Calories: 323, Sodium: 433 mg, Dietary Fiber: 2.9 g, Fat: 9.2 g, Carbs: 16.4 g, Protein: 37 g

Butternut Cauliflower Soup

Nothing hits the spot like this delicious warm Butternut Cauliflower Soup. With a hint of spice and cream, you can whip this up in no time and portion it out for the week to come.

Servings 6

Cook time 40 minutes

Ingredients

1 onion, diced

1 tsp. olive oil

3 garlic cloves, minced

1 lb. cauliflower, chopped

1 lb. butternut squash, cubed

2 cups chicken or vegetable broth

1/4 tsp. nutmeg

1/2 tsp. dried thyme

1/2 tsp. red pepper flakes

1/4 tsp. sea salt

1/2 cup half and half

1/2 cup sour cream

shredded cheddar cheese, for serving

crumbled bacon, for serving

sour cream, for serving

Instructions

1. Set to SAUTE and add olive oil and onion; cook 5 minutes. Add garlic and cook 2 minutes.

2. Fold in cauliflower, butternut squash, broth, and spices.

3. Cook on SOUP for 25 minutes.

4. Add half & half and sour cream to inner pot. Use an immersion blender to cream the soup or allow soup to cool and blend in batches in a food processor or blender until smooth.

5. Top with cheese, bacon, and additional sour cream and serve.

Nutritional Info: Calories: 150, Sodium: 378 mg, Dietary Fiber: 3.9 g, Fat: 7.8 g, Carbs: 17.2 g, Protein: 5.4 g

Pho

A taste sensation, and super healthy, Pho is a delicious Asian inspired build your own soup. This recipe will have you cooking it in the comfort of home in and no time.

Ingredients

4 lb. of beef bones

2 medium onions, sliced in half

2 cloves garlic, peeled and halved

2 medium carrots, sliced in half

1/2 cup fresh ginger

1 tbsp. apple cider vinegar

1 tsp. ground cinnamon

1 tsp. ground coriander

1 tsp. whole black peppercorns

2 tsp. sea salt

4 whole star anise

6 cups of water

Add-ins:

1 cup bean sprouts

1/2 lb. sirloin steak, sliced very thinly

1 lime, cut into wedges

2 scallions, sliced thinly

1 package of rice noodles

1 tbsp. fresh cilantro or mint

Fresh Hot Red Pepper, sliced

Instructions

1. Bring water to boil in the rice cooker. Add the bones and cook for 5 minutes.

2. Place onion, garlic, carrot, and ginger on a greased sheet-tray. Broil in the oven for 10 minutes, or until charred.

3. Add charred veggies, apple cider vinegar, spices, and more water, if needed, to cover the bones in the inner pot.

4. Lock lid in place and STEAM for 45 minutes. After cycle turns to KEEP WARM leave to rest, covered, for 15 minutes.

5. Cook the rice noodles by package instructions and set aside until ready to eat.

6. Strain the broth through a mesh strainer until it runs clear; about 3 times. Discard bones and veggies.

7. Return broth to inner pot on STEAM for 5 minutes.

8. Distribute bone broth, evenly into bowls, add in desired toppings, and enjoy!

Nutritional Info: Calories: 0, Sodium: 0 mg, Dietary Fiber: 0 g, Fat: 0 g, Carbs: 0 g, Protein: 0 g.

Beef and Guinness Stew

Whether you're Irish or not, you'll fall in love with this beef and Guinness stew. A hearty stick-to-your-ribs treat, this recipe cooks in less time than the traditional stew for a wonderful weekend meal.

Servings 8

Cook time 2 hours

Ingredients

1 lbs. stew beef, precut in 1-inch pieces

salt and pepper to season

2 tsp. olive oil

1 small sweet onion, chopped

1 tsp. garlic powder

2 large carrots, peeled and chopped into thick slices

2 celery stalks, chopped into thick pieces

4 red potatoes, quartered

1/4 cup plain flour

2 cups stout beer, like Guinness

3 tbsp. tomato paste

2 cups beef broth

1 tsp. dried thyme

Instructions

1. Season beef generously with salt and pepper.

2. Heat olive oil in the inner pot and add beef; STEAM until browned. Transfer to a plate.

3. Add onion and sauté 5 minutes. Add the carrots, celery, and potatoes, and cook for an additional 5 minutes.

4. Stir the flour into the vegetables in the inner pot and coat them evenly. Cook, stirring occasionally, for an additional 3 minutes.

5. Gently fold the Guinness into the stew; mix well to dissolve flour, then add the tomato paste, broth and thyme, scraping off any browned bits on the bottom of the inner pot with a wooden spoon or spatula.

6.   Press MEAT/STEW to cook for 5 minutes. Fold the beef back into the pot cover and cook 1 hour.

Nutritional Info: Calories: 235, Sodium: 222 mg, Dietary Fiber: 3 g, Fat: 5.2 g, Carbs: 26.4 g, Protein: 17 g

---

Beef Barley Soup

If you're looking for a soup that will keep you full until dinner this beef barley soup is just the right recipe. Full of delicious ingredients and a warm touch, you'll want to enjoy this recipe every day of the week.

Servings 6-8

Cook time 1 hour 30 minutes

Ingredients

1 lb. stew meat

Sea salt and pepper, to season stew meat

1 tsp. olive oil

10 button mushrooms, quartered

1/2 cup onion, chopped

1/2 cup celery, chopped

1/2 cup carrots, chopped

6 garlic cloves, minced

6 cups beef or vegetable broth

1 cup water

2 bay leaves

1/2 teaspoon dried thyme

2/3 cups pearl barley, rinsed

Instructions

1. Season the stew meat with sea salt and pepper. Heat olive oil in the inner pot on STEAM. Add the stew meat and brown on all sides for about 3-5 minutes.

2. Add remaining ingredients and lock lid into place.

3. SOUP for 20 minutes, serve and enjoy!

Nutritional Info: Calories: 251, Sodium: 627 mg, Dietary Fiber: 3.4 g, Fat: 9.4 g, Carbs: 17 g, Protein: 24 g

Creamy Tomato Soup

Nothing hits the spot like a bowl of creamy tomato soup. This delicious soup can beserved with Parmesan crisps or your favorite soup crackers. It's also great with a traditional grilled cheese.

Servings 6

Cook time 25 minutes

Ingredients

3 shallots, peeled and halved

1 tbsp. olive oil

3 carrots, peeled and chopped

1 (15 oz.) can tomato sauce

1 (15 oz.) can stewed tomatoes

1 tbsp. tomato paste

1 cup vegetable broth

1 tsp. oregano

1/4 tsp. sea salt

3 oz. half and half

salt and pepper to taste

Instructions

1. Add olive oil, shallots and carrot to inner pot and SAUTE for 5 minutes.

2. Add remaining ingredients and set to SOUP for 20 minutes.

3. Add the half & half to the soup and puree using an immersion blender until smooth; alternatively, allow to cool and use a food processor or blender to smooth in small batches.

4. Top with parmesan crisps or serve with your favorite soup crackers!

Nutritional Info: Calories: 90, Sodium: 610 mg, Dietary Fiber: 2.9 g, Fat: 4.5 g, Carbs: 11.8 g, Protein: 3.3 g

Potato Leek Soup

Nothing hits the spot in the winter time like a traditional potato leek soup. With a touch of cream and a pinch of nutmeg, this potato leek soup recipe is right up your alley if you love potatoes and leeks.

Servings 6-8

Cook time 30 minutes

Ingredients:

1 leek, white and light green parts only, rinsed and diced

2 tbsp. olive oil

2 cloves garlic, minced

1/2 tsp. sea salt

1/2 tsp. black pepper

1/4 teaspoon thyme

Pinch of nutmeg

3 small baking potatoes, peeled and diced

3 cups chicken or vegetable broth

1/4 cup half and half

1/4 cup sour cream

Instructions

1. Add the leek, olive oil, garlic, salt, pepper, thyme, nutmeg, broth, and potatoes to the inner pot and SOUP for 30 minutes.

2. Add half & half and sour cream. Blend with an immersion blender until smooth, and garnish with additional black pepper.

Nutritional Info: Calories: 126, Sodium: 419 mg, Dietary Fiber: 1.2 g, Fat: 6.5 g, Carbs: 14.3 g, Protein: 3.8 g

11

DESSERTS

Self-Saucing Banana Pudding

If you're looking for an easy sweet treat, this self-saucing banana bread pudding is the one for you. Simple and easy to make you'll have delicious banana pudding in just about an hour.

Servings 6-8

Cook time 1 hour

Ingredients

1 cup caster sugar

1 1/2 cups self-rising flour, sifted

1/3 cup butter, melted and cooled

1 tsp. vanilla extract

1/4 cup mashed banana

1 egg, lightly beaten

3/4 cups milk

1/2 cup packed brown sugar

1/8 tsp. nutmeg

1 tsp. cinnamon

2 1/2 cups boiling water

ice cream, to serve

Instructions

1. Preheat rice cooker to STEAM for 10 minutes.

2. Grease the inner pot with butter using wax paper.

3. Combine the first 7 ingredients above in a large mixing bowl; whisk until well-combined.

4. Fold into the inner pot. Sift sugar, nutmeg, and cinnamon over the pudding mix.

5. Spoon the boiling water gently and evenly over the mixture.

6. Lock lid in place and cook on STEAM for 1 hour.

7. Serve hot with a scoop of ice cream on top!

Nutritional Info: Calories: 307, Sodium: 76 mg, Dietary Fiber: 0.9 g, Fat: 9 g, Carbs: 54.3 g, Protein: 4 g

Chocolate Lava Cake

For chocolate lovers at heart, check out this chocolate lava cake. Easy to make and absolutely decadent, you'll be raving about this dessert for weeks.

Servings 6-8

Cook time 1 hour 10 minutes

Ingredients

1 box of Devil's Food Chocolate Cake mix, prepared according to box instructions

1 (15 oz.) can of milk chocolate frosting, divided

Non-stick cooking spray

Instructions

1. Spray the inner pot of the rice cooker with cooking spray.

2. Add cake batter prepared as instructed on the box.

3. Spoon half of the chocolate frosting into the middle of the cake batter.

4. Cook on CAKE for 1 hour.

5. Plip the inner pot upside down over a cake plate. Heat the remaining frosting in a microwave for 25 seconds, and pour over the warm cake, and serve.

Nutritional Info: Calories: 172, Sodium: 91 mg, Dietary Fiber: 0.7 g, Fat: 7.6 g, Carbs: 27 g, Protein: 0.3 g

Banana Bread

Traditionally a warm winter treat, this nutty banana bread is absolutely delicious. Of course, if you have a nut allergy simply omit the walnuts and you'll have a deliciously enjoyable banana bread treat.

Servings 6-8

Cook time 1 hour 10 minutes

Ingredients

1 1/2 cup unbleached flour

1/2 cup sugar or sugar substitute

2 tsp. baking powder

1/2 tsp. baking soda

1/2 tsp. vanilla extract

1/2 tsp. sea salt

1 cup ripe bananas, mashed

1/3 cup softened butter

1/4 cup milk

1 egg

1/4 cup walnuts, chopped

Instructions

1. Combine the flour, sugar, baking powder, baking soda and salt in a large mixing bowl; whisk until the ingredients are well mixed.

2. Fold in the bananas, butter, milk, egg and vanilla extract. Use an electric mixer to mix until the batter has a uniform thick consistency.

3. Fold in chopped walnuts.

4. Grease the bottom of the inner pot with non-stick cooking spray.

5. Pour batter into inner pot and cook on RICE for 1 hour. Transfer to plate and let cool for one hour before serving.

Nutritional Info: Calories: 255, Sodium: 211 mg, Dietary Fiber: 1.4 g, Fat: 11 g, Carbs: 36.1 g, Protein: 4.6 g

Poached Pomegranate Spiced Pears

Nothing says Christmas time or the holidays like poached pomegranate spiced pears. This delicious warm dessert is something that is sure to become a family favorite and maybe even a tradition!

Servings 4

Cook time 55 minutes

Ingredients

2 firm Anjou or Bosc pears, peeled, halved, and cored

2 cups pomegranate juice

2 cups apple cider

2 cinnamon sticks

1 large orange peel, about 1 inch thick

2 whole cloves

1 pinch of freshly shaved nutmeg

1 piece fresh ginger peeled, cut into thin slivers

Instructions

1. Add all ingredients to the inner pot of the rice cooker.

2. Lock the lid and cook on RICE for 50 minutes, or tender when a fork is inserted. Open the lid and flip the pears over; let rest for 1 hour. Turn pears over again and let sit for another hour.

3. Serve warm or refrigerate overnight for a more intense flavor and color.

Nutritional Info: Calories: 163, Sodium: 15 mg, Dietary Fiber: 5.2 g, Fat: 1.7 g, Carbs: 39.3 g, Protein: 0.9 g

Rice Cooker Tatin Cake
(Apple Upside Down Cake)

When it comes to creating a dessert found in the finest bakeries, this rice cooker tatin cake is just the treat for you. Simple and sweet, you'll fall in love with this decadent dessert.

Servings 4

Cook time

Ingredients

2 apples, peeled and cut into 8 wedges

2 tbsp. butter, plus 3 tbsp. melted

3 tbsp. sugar, plus 1/4 cup

Olive oil

1/2 cup all-purpose, unbleached flour

1 tsp. baking powder

Pinch of salt

2 eggs

Instructions

1.   Heat 2 tbsp. butter in a nonstick pan and add the apples; toss to coat and cook for about 5 minutes.

2.   Add 3 tbsp. sugar, gently stir to combine and cook until caramelized.

3.   Grease the inner pot with a drop of olive oil and add the apples to cover the bottom of the inner pot.

4.   Mix all-purpose flour, 1/4 cup sugar, baking powder, salt, 3 tbsp melted butter and the two eggs together, and pour the batter over the apples.

5.   Cook on CAKE for 60 to 90 minutes; or until firm.

6.   Allow it to cool in the inner pot for 20 minutes after cooking.

Nutritional Info: Calories: 289, Sodium: 74 mg, Dietary Fiber: 3.6 g, Fat: 8.5 g, Carbs: 49 g, Protein: 6.4 g

Green Tea Matcha Cake

For those who are looking for dessert, that's a little bit different, this green tea matcha cake is just the recipe for you. Not too sweet and packed with antioxidants your family will rave over this delicious dessert.

Servings 4-6

Cook time 1 hour 30 minutes

Ingredients

2 large eggs

1 cup unbleached flour

1/2 cup sugar

1/2 cup butter

1 tbsp. green tea matcha powder

1/2 teaspoon baking powder

Instructions

1. Combine all of the ingredients in a large mixing bowl

2. Grease the inner pot of the rice cooker with non-stick cooking spray.

3. Set to CAKE for 1 hour 30 minutes.

4. Transfer to a plate to cool for 20 minutes and serve!

Nutritional Info: Calories: 298, Sodium: 133 mg, Dietary Fiber: 2.2 g, Fat: 17.2 g, Carbs: 32.9 g, Protein: 6.4 g

Rice Pudding

Rice pudding is simple and sweet and easy to make in your MultiPot. Of course, this dessert isn't the traditional rice pudding you might be used to. We've added a Twist of Thailand for something absolutely to die for!

Servings

Cook time

Ingredients

2/3 cups Jasmine rice, uncooked

4 cups milk

1/3 cup sugar

1 tsp. vanilla extract

1 tsp. sugar

1/4 cup unsweetened coconut, shredded

Diced mango, for serving

Instructions

1. Add the rice and milk to the inner pot of the rice cooker and stir to combine.

2. Lock the lid in place and set to RICE.

3. When the Keep Warm cycle turns on, open the rice cooker, and add the sugar and vanilla; stir until well-combined.

4. Return lid and set for a second RICE cycle. Stir every 15 to 20 minutes until the desired consistency is reached.

5. Fold in the coconut. Serve warm with diced mango on top.

Nutritional Info: Calories: 0, Sodium: 0 mg, Dietary Fiber: 0 g, Fat: 0 g, Carbs: 0 g, Protein: 0 g

Lemon Lime Polenta Cake with Yogurt Icing

For those on the Mediterranean or gluten-free diet, this lemon-lime polenta cake with yogurt icing is right up your alley. Simple and sweet, you can omit the icing sugar for something a little bit more diabetic dessert friendly.

Servings 6-8

Cook time 45 minutes

Ingredients

7/8 cups almond flour

1 2/3 stick butter

1/2 cup polenta

1 1/2 tsp. baking powder

Pinch of salt

3 eggs

2 lemons

1 lime

1 tsp. vanilla extract

1 cup vanilla yogurt, for icing

1 cup icing sugar, for icing

Instructions

1. Beat butter and sugar together in a mixing bowl until creamed. Fold in eggs. Next, fold in almond flour, salt, and polenta.

2. Remove the beaters and zest the limes and lemons directly into the bowl. Add the juice of 1 lemon and lime.

3. Stir well to combine; fold the mixture into a greased inner pot, smoothing it out on top.

4. Cook on CAKE for about 30-35 minutes, or until a toothpick inserted comes out clean.

5. Set the inner pot with cake aside to cool for 20 minutes.

6. Prepare to ice by mixing yogurt and sugar together in a small mixing bowl; refrigerate to set until cake is cool.

7. Drizzle cake with icing and serve.

Nutritional Info: Calories: 337, Sodium: 203 mg, Dietary Fiber: 1.4 g, Fat: 22.7 g, Carbs: 28.9 g, Protein: 5.7 g

Chocolate Fondue

Another chocolate lover's dream, this delicious dessert is great for parties and sharing. If you love things like Tapas, you will absolutely fall in love with this chocolate fondue made right in your rice cooker.

Servings 10-20

Cook time 10 minutes

Ingredients

1/2 cup water

1/2 cup half and half

1 tbsp. honey

1/4 tsp almond extract

6 oz. 70% cacao, grated

3 oz. milk chocolate, grated

1 cup of strawberries

1 cup apples, sliced

1 cup Angel Food Cake, cubed

1 cup brownies, cubed

Instructions

1. Combine the first 4 ingredients in the rice cooker on STEAM for about 5 minutes.

2. Fold in chocolate and stir until all chocolate is melted and mixture turns glossy; about 5 minutes.

3. Keep warm to serve with strawberries, apples, angel food cake, brownies or whatever you love to dip in Chocolate Fondue!

Nutritional Info: Calories: 212, Sodium: 133 mg, Dietary Fiber: 1.4 g, Fat: 11 g, Carbs: 26.9 g, Protein: 3.6 g

Japanese Mochi

Japanese Mochi is a great dessert for those who don't like a lot of sugar. This sweet brown rice dessert topped with cocoa powder and served with ice cream gently hits the sweet tooth spot.

Servings 4-6

Cook time 11 hours 10 minutes

Ingredients

1 cup sweet brown rice

1/8 tsp. salt

1 part cornstarch, for dusting

1 part cocoa powder, for dusting

Ice cream, for serving

Instructions

1. Soak the rice in water overnight. Drain off excess water and process the rice until it makes a smooth, creamy paste in a food processor or blender.

2. Add to the inner pot of the rice cooker, lock the lid in place, and STEAM for 10 minutes until rice is glutinous sticky and glossy.

3. Combine cornstarch and cocoa powder. Dust a cookie sheet with the powder mixture.

4. Pour the hot mochi mixture onto the cookie sheet evenly; let cool for 30 minutes; then, refrigerate for 2 hours.

5. Cut the sheet of mochi into 2-inch squares and bake at 450 degrees Fahrenheit for about 10 minutes; the mochi will puff so don't be alarmed when they change shape.

6. Serve warm with a scoop of ice cream.

Nutritional Info: Calories: 161, Sodium: 53 mg, Dietary Fiber: 2.1 g, Fat: 1.2 g, Carbs: 35.3 g, Protein: 2.9 g

Easy Flan

For those who love flan, you can whip it up easy in your rice cooker in no time. You will love this easy decadent recipe that creates flawless flan in almost half the conventional time.

Servings 3-5

Cook time 1 hour 10 minutes

Ingredients:

6 egg yolks

1 (12 oz.) can evaporated milk

1 (12 oz.) can condensed milk

1 tsp. pure vanilla extract

1/4 cup granulated sugar, for caramel sauce

One flan molder

Instructions

1. Gently combine the egg yolk, condensed milk, evaporated milk and vanilla in a large mixing bowl and set aside.

2. Add granulated sugar to a saucepan and heat on a stove at medium-low; turn off the heat and assemble flan.

3. Pour the custard into the flan molder. Add caramel sauce evenly over custard. Place flan in the steamer basket.

4. Lock lid in place and set to STEAM for one hour. Let it cool completely, transfer to a plate, and serve!

Nutritional Info: Calories: 414, Sodium: 168 mg, Dietary Fiber: 0 g, Fat: 16.5 g, Carbs: 54.7 g, Protein: 13.3 g

12

KID-FRIENDLY RECIPES

Chili Mac

Chili mac is a delicious dish the kids will love. Don't forget to include them while you're cooking, to teach them the ins and outs and the healthy ways to getting around the kitchen.

Servings 4-6

Cook time 30 minutes

Ingredients

1 lb. lean ground round beef

2 tbsp. chili powder

1 tsp. garlic powder

2 cups water

1 (15 oz.) can diced tomatoes

1 (15 oz.) can red kidney beans, in chili sauce

2 cups elbow macaroni

1 cup cheddar cheese, shredded

Instructions

1. Preheat the rice cooker on STEAM for five minutes. Add beef and sauté until browned; breaking it up with a wooden spatula while cooking.

2. Stir in the chili powder and garlic powder.

3. Add the water, tomatoes, red kidney beans, and pasta.

4. Lock lid in place and cook for one RICE cycle.

5. Serve immediately, topped with cheese.

Nutritional Info: Calories: 761, Sodium: 258 mg, Dietary Fiber: 13.4 g, Fat: 30.6 g, Carbs: 69.1 g, Protein: 53.3 g

Mac N' Cheese

Mac and cheese is a kid-friendly, fan favorite when it comes to delicious dishes. You can't go wrong when you're whipping up this old favorite in the rice cooker. A great choice for the kids.

Servings 4

Cook time 50 minutes

Ingredients

2 cups elbow macaroni

1 tsp. sea salt

1 (12 oz.) can evaporated milk

3/4 cups cheddar cheese, shredded

3/4 cups shaved parmesan cheese

3/4 cups mozzarella melting cheese, like Velveeta Shreds

1/2 teaspoon mustard powder

1/2 teaspoon freshly ground black pepper

2 tbsp. Butter

Salt and pepper, to taste

Instructions

1. Combine the macaroni, salt and 2 cups water in the rice cooker. Set on RICE and cook for 30 minutes as water is absorbed.

2. Fold in the butter, milk, cheese, salt, and pepper.

3. Lock the lid, turn the rice cooker to KEEP WARM and let cook, stirring occasionally for 10 minutes. Serve warm!

Nutritional Info: Calories: 486, Sodium: 1021 mg, Dietary Fiber: 1.5 g, Fat: 25.2 g, Carbs: 41.2 g, Protein: 23.5 g

Spaghetti and Meatballs

If you're looking for dinner in a dash, this 20-minute spaghetti and meatballs are absolutely delicious. This one-pot dish is also great for those who don't have time to throw a meal together. Simply put everything in the pot and hit delayed timer and you've got a one-pot instant meal when you get home.

Servings 4

Cook Time 20 minutes

Ingredients

1 (15 oz.) can of Italian Sauce or marinara

3 1/2 cup water

1/2 lb. spaghetti pasta

1 lb. frozen meatballs (1/2 inch size)

1 tsp. garlic powder

1 tsp. dried Italian herbs

Parmesan cheese, for serving

Garlic toast, for serving

Instructions

1. Combine all ingredients in the inner pot.

2. Lock lid in place and set to RICE for 20 minutes.

3. Serve immediately with parmesan cheese and garlic toast.

Nutritional Info: Calories: 492, Sodium: 1010 mg, Dietary Fiber: 2.3 g, Fat: 28.3 g, Carbs: 31.5 g, Protein: 19.7 g

Applesauce

Applesauce is a delicious snack alternative that you can make right in your own kitchen with your rice cooker. No more cooking apples for hours, you can do it in just 30 minutes with this amazing recipe.

Servings 4-6

Cook time 30 minutes

Ingredients

4 large apples, peeled, cored and chopped

2 tsp. sugar

1/4 cup unfiltered apple juice

3/4 tsp. ground cinnamon

Directions:

1. Add all ingredients into the inner pot of the rice cooker.

2. Lock lid in place and cook on RICE for 25 to 30 minutes.

3. Puree with hand blender or food processor and serve warm or chill in refrigerator overnight in a resealable container.

Nutritional Info: Calories: 89, Sodium: 1 mg, Dietary Fiber: 3.7 g, Fat: 0.3 g, Carbs: 23.6 g, Protein: 0.5 g

Baked Beans

Baked beans are a great side dish for cookouts and picnics, or something fun in the summertime. It's also a great dish for the whole family when it comes to cooking for picky kids.

Servings 4-6

Cook time 35 minutes

Ingredients

1 1/2 cup dry pinto beans

1 cup warm water

2 tbsp. olive oil

1 medium sweet onion, finely diced

1/4 teaspoon salt

1 tsp. garlic powder

1 (15 oz.) can tomato sauce

2 tbsp. ketchup

1 tbsp. brown sugar

1/2 teaspoon paprika

1/8 teaspoon nutmeg

2 bay leaves

Instructions

1. Add dried beans to a large bowl and fill up with double the water. Mix in a teaspoon of salt and soak overnight. Strain and rinse; add to inner pot.

2. Add remaining ingredients to inner pot, lock lid in place and set to BEANS for 25 minutes. Test bean texture, if not cooked to desired softness continue cooking in 10-minute increments until done.

3. Serve alone or with your favorite cookout food!

Nutritional Info: Calories: 247, Sodium: 532 mg, Dietary Fiber: 9.2 g, Fat: 5.5 g, Carbs: 39.3 g, Protein: 11.7 g

Corn On The Cob

Corn on the cob is another great snack or side dish when it comes to cooking for children who might be a bit picky. This delicious corn on the cob recipe is cooked to perfection in just 25 minutes with the MultiPot.

Servings 3-6

Cook time 25 minutes

Ingredients

3 ears of corn, husked and rinsed, cut in half

Butter, for serving

Salt, for serving

Instructions

1. Fill the inner pot with 2 cups water.
2. Place corn on the cob in the steamer basket; insert basket into the rice cooker.
3. Lock lid and STEAM for 25 minutes.
4. Enjoy with butter and salt to taste!

Nutritional Info: Calories: 144, Sodium: 23 mg, Dietary Fiber: 4.2 g, Fat: 3.2 g, Carbs: 29 g, Protein: 5 g

Bacon Ranch Potatoes

If you're looking for something else the kids might love, you can whip up these bacon ranch potatoes in no time on the weekday. It's the delicious alternative to plain roasted potatoes, these potatoes are tangy and pack a mean side dish punch!

Servings 6

Cook time 25 minutes

Ingredients

2 lb. red potatoes, rinsed and cleaned, cut into 1-inch pieces

3 bacon strips, cut into pieces

2 tsp. dried parsley

1 tsp. garlic powder

1 cup cheddar cheese, shredded

1 package ranch dressing seasoning

Instructions

1. Add potatoes, bacon and 1/4 cup of water into the inner pot of rice cooker.

2. Stir in parsley and garlic powder.

3. Set to RICE for 25 minutes; check potatoes. Add additional water if needed to cook longer.

4. Transfer potatoes to a mixing bowl and combine with ranch dressing and cheese; serve immediately.

Nutritional Info: Calories: 191, Sodium: 163 mg, Dietary Fiber: 2.7 g, Fat: 7.2 g, Carbs: 24.8 g, Protein: 7.9 g

Sloppy Joes

Sloppy joes are a lovely traditional treat for kids when it comes to a hearty lunch. You can cook sloppy joes in the comfort of your own home, using your rice cooker in just under 40 minutes with this delicious recipe.

Servings 6

Cook time 35 minutes

INGREDIENTS

2 lbs. lean ground beef

1 small onions, diced

1 small green bell pepper, diced

1 tsp. garlic powder

2 tsp. cumin

2 tsp. paprika

1 tsp. salt

1/2 tsp. black pepper

1 (15 oz) can tomato sauce

2 tbsp. tomato puree

2 tsp. apple cider vinegar

2 tsp. molasses

2 tsp. Yellow mustard

1 tsp. ketchup

6 sandwich buns

Instructions

1. Brown beef in a skillet over medium heat. Drain. Combine all ingredients in the inner pot of the rice cooker and MEAT for 20 minutes.

2. Let rest for 5 minutes to set.

3. Spoon onto sandwich buns and serve with your favorite sides!

Nutritional Info: Calories: 191, Sodium: 163 mg, Dietary Fiber: 2.7 g, Fat: 7.2 g, Carbs: 24.8 g, Protein: 7.9 g

Homemade Chicken Soup

If your children love chicken soup, forget the can and create a homemade treat for the whole family. This delicious soup warms your soul on any day of the year.

Servings 8

Cook time 35 minutes

Ingredients

2 carrots, peeled and sliced

2 celery stalks, trimmed, rinsed and sliced

1 small yellow onion, peeled and diced

5 garlic cloves, peeled and diced

2 quarts chicken broth

1 cup water

2 tablespoons apple cider vinegar

2 cans chicken, drained

1 package egg noodles

Instructions

1. Add all ingredients to the inner pot.

2. Lock lid in place and set to SOUP for 30 minutes.

3. Leave on KEEP WARM for 5 minutes or until ready to serve. Serve with grilled cheese or your favorite soup crackers.

Nutritional Info: Calories: 133, Sodium: 802 mg, Dietary Fiber: 0.9 g, Fat: 2.9 g, Carbs: 9 g, Protein: 16.3 g

Pizza Pasta

Forget ordering pizza, just whip up this yummy dish in not time. Pizza Pasta is absolutely delicious and will definitely become a kid/family favorite.

Servings 4-6

Cook time 35 minutes

Ingredients:

1 tbsp. olive oil

2 (8 oz.) jars of pizza sauce

3 1/2 cups water

1 (8 oz.) package mozzarella cheese shredded

1 cup pepperoni slices

2 cups macaroni

2 tsp. garlic powder

1 tsp. Italian seasoning

Instructions

1. Combine olive oil, pasta, water and 1 jar of pizza sauce in the inner pot. Cook on STEAM for 15 minutes.

2. Fold in the additional jar of sauce, half of the cheese and half pepperoni. Cook on STEAM for an additional 10 minutes.

3. Top with remaining cheese and pepperoni; Cook on STEAM for 5 minutes or until cheese is melted and serve.

Nutritional Info: Calories: 404, Sodium: 936 mg, Dietary Fiber: 2.3 g, Fat: 21.2 g, Carbs: 31.8 g, Protein: 21.4 g

Lasagna

No more baking lasagna for hours, or boiling noodles, and spending loads of time on what your kids love. You can whip up an easy lasagna dish right in your rice cooker in no time.

Servings 6

Cook time 30 minutes

Ingredients

1 (16 oz.) package pasta, like ruffles or spirals

1 cup ricotta cheese

1 cup mozzarella cheese

1 lb. ground beef

1 (32 oz.) jar pasta sauce

4 cups water

Instructions

1. Add beef to inner pot and brown on steam until cooked through.

2. Add pasta, sauce, and water; cook on STEAM for 20 minutes.

3. Stir in Ricotta cheese and half the mozzarella.

4. Pour into a baking pan and top with the remaining mozzarella.

5. Broil for 2-3 minutes in an oven or until cheese is melted and serve.

Nutritional Info: Calories: 540, Sodium: 881 mg, Dietary Fiber: 3.9 g, Fat: 15.5 g, Carbs: 58.9 g, Protein: 39.7 g

Pizza Pull-Apart Bread

This delicious bread is a great afternoon snack or after-school snack for the kids. They'll fall in love with this pizza that they can pull apart and dip into their favorite sauce.

Servings 4-6

Cook Time 10 minutes

Ingredients

2 cans pizza dough, like Pillsbury

1/3 cup olive oil

2 cups mozzarella cheese

1 tsp. garlic powder

1/4 cup parmesan cheese grated

4 cloves garlic minced

1 package of mini pepperonis

pizza sauce, for serving

Instructions

1. Cut pizza dough into 1-inch strips.

2. Toss all ingredients in a large mixing bowl using your hands.

3. Add 1 cup of water to the bottom of your inner pot.

4. Place dough in a springform pan and place over water in the inner pot.

5. Cook on STEAM for 15 minutes. Let stand on KEEP WARM for 5 minutes and serve with a pizza sauce for dipping.

Nutritional Info: Calories: 283, Sodium: 570 mg, Dietary Fiber: 0.6 g, Fat: 20.9 g, Carbs: 18.2 g, Protein: 6.9 g

Chili Dogs

Nothing beats a great chili dog, except maybe this recipe. If your kids are in love with hot dogs, you'll really enjoy this delicious recipe that can be cooked in just under 10 minutes.

Servings 4-8

Cook time 9 minutes

Ingredients

1 package uncured hot dogs

1 package hot dog buns

1 (10 oz.) can hot dog chili

Ketchup, for serving

Mustard, for serving

Instructions

1. Add hot dog chili to inner pot. Add hot dogs to the steam basket and place above the inner pot.

2. Lock lid in place and STEAM for 5-7 minutes.

3. Assemble dogs in buns and top with chili, ketchup, and mustard.

Nutritional Info: Calories: 177, Sodium: 539 mg, Dietary Fiber: 2.1 g, Fat: 4.7 g, Carbs: 26.8 g, Protein: 6.3 g